SELF-IMPROVEMENT PUZZLES

IMPROVE YOUR MEMORY

PRACTICAL PUZZLES TO INCREASE MEMORY POWER

Bath · New York · Cologne · Melbourne · Delhi
Hong Kong · Shenzhen · Singapore

This edition published by Parragon Books Ltd in 2017

Parragon Books Ltd
Chartist House
15–17 Trim Street
Bath BA1 1HA, UK
www.parragon.com

Copyright © Parragon Books Ltd 2017
Written and designed by Any Puzzle Media Ltd

All pictures from Shutterstock.com

ISBN 978-1-4748-8138-8

Printed in China

CONTENTS

CHAPTER 1: INTRODUCTION

About This Book 5
Can You Improve Your Memory? 6
Memory Training 8

CHAPTER 2: INTRODUCTION TO MEMORY

Memorable Moments 10
Forgotten Facts 14

CHAPTER 3: TYPES OF MEMORY

Short-term Memory 16
Long-term Memory 20
Procedural Memory 24

CHAPTER 4: HOW TO REMEMBER

The Importance of Repetition 26
The Importance of Paying Attention 30
Connecting Memories 32
Taking Note of Memories 36

CHAPTER 5: BASIC MEMORY TECHNIQUES

Acronyms 40
Acrostics 44
Related Facts 48

CHAPTER 6: FURTHER MEMORY TECHNIQUES

Chunking Memory 52
Visualization of Memories 56
Poetry and Sound 60

CHAPTER 7: USING YOUR MEMORY

Basic Number Memorization 64
Remembering Names and Faces 68
Remembering Passages of Text 72

CHAPTER 8: ADVANCED MEMORY TECHNIQUES

Memory Palaces 76
Memory Pegs 80
Memory Palaces with Added Pegs 84

CHAPTER 9: SPECIFIC MEMORY METHODS

Advanced Number Memorization 88
Remembering Usernames and Passwords 92
Everyday Memory 96

CHAPTER 10: CHALLENGE YOUR MEMORY

Fresh Challenges 100

CHAPTER 11: SOLUTIONS

Solutions 110

ABOUT THIS BOOK

Our memory is central to everything we do. Without it, we'd forget what we just did, what we were planning to do, and even what we were in the middle of doing.

We all have similar memory capabilities, but what differs from person to person is how much we take conscious advantage of them. With just a few simple methods, you can improve your memory so that you no longer forget passwords or PINs. You'll never forget a train time, a gate at the airport or hotel room number ever again.

This book provides a practical guide to using your memory. It isn't a reference book, designed to teach you interesting facts about what's going on upstairs. Instead, it focuses entirely on things that are directly *useful* to you in your everyday life. All of the content is presented in a practical way, so you can apply it immediately on a day-to-day basis.

We'll look at a wide range of techniques, from the basic through to the advanced, for memorizing material effectively and easily – and for maintaining those memories for whatever period of time you might require them.

Throughout the book are many puzzles and exercises, all related to the material that they immediately follow. Try not to skip those that seem tricky – these are probably the ones that will provide the most benefit!

The book is broken into chapters, each consisting of a small number of separate sections. The chapters are best read in order, although the book is also designed so you can dip in and out to some extent – but you'll get the most benefit by reading through in the order given. The memory exercises, where relevant, have solutions at the back of the book, if you need them.

CAN YOU IMPROVE YOUR MEMORY?

Unless you're an actor, or in some other profession where you are expected to remember a large amount of material, then the chances are that most things you need to remember you simply write down in some way. Indeed, transferring lists of to-do items and the like from our memories down to a piece of paper, or digital item list, can be a great way of relieving the stress of worrying that we might forget! But even so, there will often be situations in which it would be much better and easier to simply remember something, rather than having to have a pen and paper, or digital device, with us at all times for taking notes.

WHAT MIGHT WE WANT TO MEMORIZE?

In some circumstances you might not be able to take immediate notes, and so will be forced to use your memory – for example if someone is giving you quick directions on the street as a favour. You want to be able to remember what they say, and not forget it. You can't reasonably expect them to wait while you write them all down and make sure you haven't forgotten anything. Or maybe you're on the phone and you're being given a list of prices that you need to remember; or perhaps you're in a meeting and you want to be able to remember your talking points, as well as what you say, without sitting there with your face in a notepad.

Perhaps the most contemporary example of all is usernames and passwords for online services – the moment you write down your bank passwords, or share your PIN with multiple accounts, you are increasing the risk of financial loss, or even identity theft. Banks often won't repay stolen money if they believe you have written down your security details, so learning to use your memory for these really is an important skill. Even if you write down some kind of hint, you still need to remember what the hint *means*.

LEARNING TO MEMORIZE INFORMATION

We so rarely explicitly test our memories nowadays that many people think that they don't have a very good memory – but the truth is that we all have pretty much the same memory. What differs is not what we *can* do with our memories, but *what* we do with them. You can, with very little effort, learn to remember long lists of items, names and faces of everyone you meet, every username and password you have, and even all the phone numbers, email addresses and birthdays of your friends, should you wish to do so.

Various memory techniques were once taught to generations of schoolchildren, who were expected to be able to recall long lists of historical and other facts. Going back not very far in history, it was the case that the majority of people could neither read nor write, so using their memories was the *only* way that stories, news and other information could be conveyed from one person to another. In classical writings from thousands of years ago, there are references to memory techniques that were regularly used by many people – it is only very recently that most of us have stopped making any attempt to learn the day-to-day information we require. Many of us may not even know the phone number of our family members, or the email addresses of our close friends – and, you might argue, why should we? Nowadays technology, or a well-organized filing system, keeps track of these things for us. Except, of course, when our phone breaks and we are out on our own, when we really do want to be sure we know at least some basic contact information for other people. So even if the amount of information we should learn to remember is much smaller than it once was, the need is still there.

Luckily, there are many simple techniques you can use to make remembering things considerably more effortless than you would probably anticipate.

MEMORY TRAINING

In this book we cover two main areas of using your memory. First, we look at the simple day-to-day things you can do to make life more memorable. And then we look at some specific methods of memorization that will help you learn certain types of fact or other information, working up from basic techniques to slightly more complex ones. The aim is simply to improve your memory for day-to-day tasks – we don't specifically look at memory feats, such as attempting to learn the order of a deck of cards or similar, although you could certainly use the techniques presented in this book to work towards this goal, should you ever wish to.

WHAT MAKES SOMETHING MEMORABLE?

We'll start by covering things that are naturally memorable, and look at why this might be and whether we can exploit this property to remember things that are much harder to learn. We'll also look at why you remember some facts just briefly, but others last many years.

When you come across new information you first shift it into what is called short-term memory, which is rapidly forgotten if not stored away as a long-term memory. So we'll look at how your ability to focus and pay attention is key to your ability to storing long-term memories, and how conscious practising helps you to learn physical memories. We'll also see that you can extend this practice method to general repetition for making memories longer-lasting, in a process called 'rehearsal'.

Throughout the book we'll look at how connecting and associating memories, both with each other and with existing memories, forms the basis of most memorization techniques. This is easily demonstrated by considering two entirely separate objects: a frying pan, and a postbox. If you want to remember these two together, either in order or just as a pair, you simply find a way to connect them. For example, you could imagine a frying pan sticking out of a postbox, or a frying pan tightly wrapped as an odd-looking parcel that is sitting by a postbox, or indeed whatever method of linking you can come up with that catches your attention or you find wryly amusing.

This associating of ideas also means that it becomes easier to retrieve a memory too. Sometimes we remember things only once we are prompted, so we look at how you can reduce the need for prompts by making memories more accessible.

MEMORY TECHNIQUES

We'll look at various specific techniques for making things more memorable. We'll start with simple methods, such as taking notes, and how best to organize and learn them, before moving on to consider acronyms, acrostics and a more general method of simply learning more about a subject to improve our retention of the key central facts.

We then go on to consider chunking, which is where we join neighbouring pieces of information together in order to reduce the total number of items we need to remember, and look at how we can use a visualization process to improve memorization. We also look at how rhymes, poetry and music can be especially memorable, and how we can use this to benefit us in day-to-day memory usage.

We'll spend some time looking at numbers, with both basic and advanced techniques for memorization, and we'll also consider names and faces, and learning passages of text such as for a presentation. Later on we'll look at passwords, PINs and everyday memory requirements such as not losing your keys.

We also look at a couple of slightly more advanced memory techniques, which despite having to spend a small amount of time learning to use will then provide incredible memory power essentially for ever more. Specifically, we consider memory palaces and then memory pegs – before combining them into one unified memorization technique.

MEMORABLE MOMENTS

What in your life do you find most memorable? There will be key moments that you will never forget, and people and places that you can always bring to mind whenever you want. Then there's a long list of countless facts you know, from your own birthday and name right through to arbitrary general knowledge about the world.

But then there's a whole host of memories we never even consciously consider, such as how to walk, what our house looks like and how to speak in our native language. If you play a musical instrument, or drive, you probably don't think about the exact actions your limbs are making as you do so, and yet these too are functions you have at some point memorized to the point where they became entirely automatic.

To remember something we need to pay conscious attention to it, but once we have learned it, recall can be entirely subconscious. Have you ever made yourself a drink and then not been able to recall whether you did or not? The action was so automatic that it was entirely unmemorable, meaning that your brain took such little note of it that you were able to forget it had even happened just moments later.

STRONG EMOTIONS

So, we need to be paying attention to remember something. Even so, we find some events or facts far more memorable than others.

Think back to major news stories in the past decades. If you were alive at the time, do you remember where you were during the moon landings, or the *Challenger* disaster, or 9/11? These events were, for many people, so momentous that they remember exactly what they were doing when they first heard about them. When a major event has occurred, we may many years later still remember where we were, who we were with, and perhaps even what we were wearing. Now the fact is that these personal memories are probably of little use to us, but our brains took great care to remember them because the emotions of that moment were so strong that it thought they might be incredibly important to us.

Obviously you can't create, or wish for, a momentous event every time you want to remember something, but the basic principle of making something meaningful or interesting to us still applies. Humour is a great example – if we find something funny then we usually find it easier to remember. Perhaps it's because it's instantly more interesting, or perhaps we have to pay a certain minimum amount of attention before we can actually get so far as finding it funny. The next time you want to remember a fact, try looking for a way to make it humorous.

MEMORABLE PEOPLE, PLACES AND THINGS

Not everyone is equally memorable, but there are two basic classes of people, place and thing that are especially memorable to us:

- Those people that we are extremely familiar with, whether it is people we see every day or have known for a very long time, or people who are extremely important to us and so we have devoted a great deal of attention to. This applies also to a lesser extent to places and objects, where the more familiar we are with something the better we remember it.

- Those people we've encountered who were especially remarkable in some way, either because they were of importance to us at some key point, or because they stood out in an unusual way. The latter, for example, could include someone dressed in a ridiculous costume that you saw only briefly, but which you found so surprising and out of place that the memory became seared into your brain. A similar process can again apply in a lesser way to places and objects as well.

YOUR MEMORIES

1. Think of a momentous event that has taken place during your lifetime, and write down a list of all of the trivia you can remember from that day. Do you recall what time of day it was, where you were, who you were with, what you were wearing, what you were doing at the time you heard, and so on? Do you even remember where you were standing or sitting in a room?

    _____

    _____

    _____

    _____

    _____

2. Can you think of any people or places you've been that were especially memorable? For each person or place, can you work out what it was that made them *so* memorable?

    _____

    _____

    _____

    _____

    _____

    _____

    _____

3. Test your initial memory skills by seeing how many of these numbers you can remember. Study them for up to a minute, then cover them over and write as many as you can in the space below. How many did you recall correctly?

17   22   19   35   46   5   13   28

_____

_____

4. Now try a similar memory test with the following objects. How many can you remember after studying them for no more than a minute?

Dog	Chair	Piano	Statue
Hosepipe	Pencil	Rope	Plant

_____

_____

_____

5. Now try the previous puzzle again, but this time using abstract words rather than objects. You may find this harder.

Clarity	Observe	Dangerous	Sleeping
Suffix	Plenty	Via	Boredom

_____

_____

_____

FORGOTTEN FACTS

Without doubt, you can remember an enormous number of things. But sometimes you also become aware of just how much you have also forgotten. Obviously there are many things you don't *want* to remember, but the more frustrating things to forget are facts that you know you once knew. Consider, for example, a subject that you enjoyed at school, and once were quite knowledgeable about. How much do you still remember? Enough to pass a school-level exam, or has the knowledge slipped out of your brain?

Many memories need to be revisited to be maintained, since if we don't make use of a memory, and our brain has no particular reason to think it is important, it may not keep hold of it – or at least, it may become much harder for us to access. Perhaps we don't forget everything entirely, but it needs a significant trigger to start recalling what we once did know. Have you ever had the experience where an unrelated comment triggered a whole flood of memories from some distant point in the past, that you had completely forgotten about?

UNFORGETTABLE FACTS

There are sure to be some facts, that are of no use to you in your day-to-day life, that you *do* continue to recall with absolute clarity. Within these, no doubt, lies the secret to remembering the facts that you actually *want* to recall. On pages 10 to 11, we already looked at some causes of memories that barely fade, but how about the rest of our lives? Perhaps we want to learn trivia, such as a list of kings and queens, or simply remember a set of birthday dates and a list of friends we want to send Christmas cards to. These may well be examples of things you could simply make a written list of instead, but what if you do want to commit them to memory?

Think about what made the facts you *do* recall memorable. For example, perhaps someone once taught you a short rhyme like the following:

> *In fourteen hundred and ninety-two,*
> *Colombus sailed the ocean blue.*

It's hardly a masterpiece, and the rhyme with 'blue' really just gives you the final digit of the four-digit year, but even so generations of school children once learned a historical fact via this miniature poem. The rhyme and phrasing make it much more memorable than it would otherwise be.

Consider the lines on a music stave. Many children are taught to learn the notes that cross each of the five lines with a simple phrase along the lines of the following:

> *Every good boy deserves fun.*

In this particular case the initial letters of the phrase give the musical notes reading up from the bottom of the stave: E, G, B, D and F. The phrase is somehow much easier to remember than the individual letters. But why is this? And why doesn't the phrase need to tell you whether the notes read *up* or *down* the stave?

MEMORIZATION METHODS

We'll return to examine the methods of memorization used by the above phrases later on, but the key point to note here is that remembering these relatively abstract facts becomes much easier when you frame them in a certain way.

Learning to better use your memory is a combination of a few factors:

- Paying proper attention to the information you wish to learn

- Rehearsing information by reminding yourself of what you learn

- Using a range of techniques to help make things easier to remember

SHORT-TERM MEMORY

Short-term memory is a term that covers anything you remember for just a few moments, and then forget.

Examples of short-term memory storage include briefly remembering a phone number as you make a note of it on a contacts list, or reading an email or web address that you immediately go and type into your browser. These aren't things you aim to remember past the immediate moments when you are using them, and therefore form the majority of our memory interactions. When adding up a series of numbers in your head, you need to remember the intermediate sums only briefly – once they've been used they're no longer of any use, and you will probably forget them almost instantly.

Immediately forgetting things may seem annoying, but it is actually essential for survival. Imagine, if you never forgot *anything*, how overwhelming it would be. Our brains have developed to keep hold of memories only if they think they are useful. If we make no conscious effort to remember something past the immediate moment we learn it then we will soon forget it, unless there is something else that makes that thing remarkable enough to remember in its own right.

There is a natural limit to how much you can hold in your short-term memory, and your brain essentially automatically gets rid of the oldest items in it. In that way it doesn't just fill up, leaving you unable to remember anything else. This is lucky, since short-term memory is also how memories are transferred to long-term memory.

SHORT-TERM MEMORY ITEM LIMITS

The duration of short-term memory is up to around 20 seconds, which means that if you pay no special attention to what's in it, in order to start transferring it to long-term memory, then it will be gone once time is up.

What's more, you can only remember around seven items at any one time. To test this, read the following numbers, as slowly as you like but without rereading them, then shut the book for 10 seconds *and don't think about them during that period* before trying to write them down, in the same order, on a piece of paper:

4   5   7   3   5   9   0   8   4   6

Did you remember up to seven of them? This might then make you wonder whether, if you could combine multiple items into a single item, you could improve your short-term memory? The answer is yes, but only to a certain extent – if you are remembering words, for example, then the longer the words the fewer you will hold in your short-term memory.

Try the same test with these five two-digit numbers:

33   46   90   17   54

You might find this slightly easier, because we have reduced the number of items to five. Although they were more complex objects to remember, the reduction in number possibly helped compensate for this.

FLUSHING YOUR SHORT-TERM MEMORY

To more directly demonstrate the item limit on your short-term memory, try reading this set of numbers below, just once, then immediately start counting backwards from 100 down to 90. Don't specifically attempt to keep the digits in your head by rehearsing them between countdown numbers. How many of the original numbers can you still recall once you reach 90?

8   0   5   6   4   7   3   4

SHORT-TERM MEMORY TESTS

Try these various memory exercises, to explore the limits of your short-term memory. In each case, see how much you can remember just by looking through a list once only, then looking away for about 10 seconds. During those 10 seconds don't make any attempt to remind yourself of the items. If you find this hard to do, try finding something to mildly distract yourself during those 10 seconds – but don't read anything, since it will flush out your short-term memory.

6. See how many of these words you can remember after 10 seconds of not thinking about them. Make a note, then check back to see:

Prince	Cloud	Mine	Paper
Sparrow	Boy	Keyboard	Politician
Dungarees	Yacht	Soup	Ceiling

7. Now see how many of these words you can remember under similar conditions – these are all abstract, rather than nouns as above:

Eternity	Slow	Dream	Reverse
Ignorance	Greed	Wistful	Laugh
Leaking	Pale	Under	Twisting

8. Remembering two-digit numbers is often tricky, so now try:

35	47	23	98
76	64	77	54
45	17	03	26

9. See how many of these pictures you can recall after 10 seconds has passed – then make a quick note on a bit of paper to describe each image, then check to see how many you got right:

10. Now read this first list of letters, take a 10-second break where you don't rehearse the list, and then see how many of the letters in the second list you can identify that were in the first list:

X	D	H	L
F	E	M	B
Q	R	P	V

S	E	P	R
Z	X	D	N
T	H	U	L

LONG-TERM MEMORY

While short-term memory contains items you forget about within a small number of seconds, long-term memory refers to everything you remember for longer. These are items that are no longer being held for your immediate attention, but are able to be retrieved at a later date or time, when you need them. Holding items in your short-term memory for longer than 20 seconds requires you to consciously reiterate them to keep them fresh, but long-term memories are maintained without any conscious effort.

Long-term memory covers everything we know, from facts and faces through to identifying the sun when we go outside. So far as we know, there is no practical limit on long-term memory. No one has ever 'run out' of storage space, and indeed we don't even know whether forgotten long-term memories are truly lost or simply become inaccessible. It must stand to reason that there is a limit, but perhaps that limit is so large that in practice we will never encounter it during our lifetimes. Indeed, it has even been shown that the brain can grow new neurons to store certain memories, as for example with London black cab drivers who must memorize 25,000 streets *plus* points of interest within half a mile of those streets, as well as hundreds of routes too.

Much of our long-term memory is stored without us consciously trying to remember it, whether that's names and faces, where the various rooms in our house are relative to one another, or what happened last week in our favourite TV show. In particular we have fantastic visual memories, and can often identify whether we have seen a particular photograph before, even if we last saw it a long time ago.

LONG-TERM MEMORY RETRIEVAL

Successfully *identifying* a photograph you have seen before is a very different task to being able to consciously *recall*, without any cue, all of the photographs you have ever seen.

This difference between recognition and recall extends across our memory. If we are asked to name all the books we have ever read, or films we've ever seen, we may come up with a list of a hundred or so, given sufficient time. And yet, if we are *given* a list of major books, or films, the chances are we will identify far more from that list than we could actively recall without prompting.

Part of the reason for this disparity in long-term memory recall is that we need a trigger to retrieve the information. The film or book took enough of our attention that our brain remembers some of the information about it, but perhaps in a self-contained way, rather than indexed in our head under 'film'. When we start accessing information related to the film, say for example if someone describes the plot to you, or you are given the title, you may then recall it perfectly well – but without any trigger, the information stays locked away.

REFRESHING MEMORIES

Some long-term memories seem to remain clear forever, whereas others fade with time. Detailed memories, such as of key family occasions, probably consist of many small linked memories, so in practice our memory of even these 'unforgettable' occasions may fade, even if we don't realize that they are doing so.

What generally does get lost, if no longer used, is very specific knowledge. Say for example you once knew many things about organic chemistry compounds, but then completely stopped using that information once you had completed a chemistry exam. In such a situation, most of that knowledge will eventually be forgotten. To maintain it we would need to use it, either by learning new facts that build on and require the retention of the existing knowledge, or by actively maintaining an interest in the subject. Rehearsing the specific facts themselves may even be needed.

LONG-TERM MEMORY TESTS

For each of the memory tests on this page, try memorizing the content and then read another page or two in the book before coming back to see what you can remember. If the information had successfully passed into your long-term memory you should be able to recall some of it.

Next, re-memorize the content and then leave it for an hour or more before attempting to recall it.

Finally, following a last attempt to ensure you can remember it, leave it overnight and see what you can recall tomorrow.

11. Memorize this list of names:

David	Jennifer	Daniel
Matthew	Owen	John
Lewis	Gareth	Peter
Theo	Xavier	Sara

Test your long-term memory in a few minutes; in an hour; and again tomorrow, as described at the top of this page.

12. Try a similar memorization task with this list of colours:

Red	White	Mauve
Ochre	Puce	Tangerine
Blue	Scarlet	Green
Sage	Silver	Aquamarine

13. Study these pictures, then see how many you can remember in a few minutes, in an hour, and then this time tomorrow:

14. See if you can memorize these pairs of letters – without any additional techniques this is harder than memorizing words:

AJ	GM	SS	XO
TX	LL	JM	BP
KL	YH	VT	ZS

15. Now try this final long-term memory test – see if you can memorize this entire nonsense poem:

Once upon a special time, I met a friend of mine,

He took me to the park one day, and planted me in soil.

I grew each spring up to the sky, an ever-climbing vine,

Dreaming all the night and day, burning midnight oil.

Despite the lack of clear sense, do the rhymes and rhythms help?

PROCEDURAL MEMORY

One form of long-term memory is procedural memory, representing all of the tasks that we can perform without any conscious memory retrieval. So while we may *consciously* be able to retrieve the fact that the Domesday Book was completed in 1086, we will be able to pick up a pencil and write without *any* conscious thought about how to form each letter and move our hand. Indeed, sometimes if we try to consciously think about exactly what we're doing, we can get confused – for example, once you have learned to drive if you try to actively think about what exactly your foot is doing you may suddenly lose the ability to drive – not that it would be wise to test this, next time you're in a car.

Procedural memories enable us to ride a bicycle, swim, walk, hop and speak. We have to explicitly learn these skills, but then as we learn them they are transferred to long-term, procedural memory.

PRACTICE

We learn physical acts of skill, from walking onwards, by building stronger and more detailed procedural memories. As we practise, so we get better – whether it's first steps as a toddler or learning to juggle, the more we work on a skill the better we become. We develop more and more procedural memories connected to the skill, improving our abilities. The procedural memories we already have are reinforced, until eventually we can perform the skill without any conscious thought. At that point we can then perhaps develop the skill further, such as from walking to running, or from juggling balls to juggling clubs.

Think about how you learned the procedural memories you have. They were skills that at first you had to practice, but which you became better at the more you tried them. The same applies to memories in general – the more you use them, and the more detailed they become, the stronger they are. If you regularly read a favourite novel, for example, then over time you will naturally start to memorize it whether you try to or not.

It also helps to pay as much attention to a task as possible. If you want to learn to play tennis, casually swinging the racket about and hoping for the best will be a slow way to learn, but actively focusing on your grip, stance, swing and power will lead to much more rapid progress. Think of how studiously a toddler concentrates on trying to walk, and the intense focus required. The more attentively you concentrate on skills you are trying to learn, the faster you will acquire them.

REHEARSING PROCEDURAL MEMORIES

Fascinatingly, procedural memories can be improved without having to physically engage in the activity. Just thinking about doing something actually helps you learn to do it, although of course some parts of the learning experience – falling over, or dropping juggling balls – cannot be learned without physical experimentation. But you can certainly practise the things you have already experienced in this way, by thinking through the physical sequence of actions you would perform.

When learning physical skills, there will be little benefit to *over*-practising them. In fact, you may even learn them less well if you don't take at least short breaks every so often. Your brain needs time to process what it has learned.

Sleep is another key component in the laying-down of long-term procedural memories. During sleep our brains run back over the events of the day, learning from them and storing memories. If you become tired your ability to remember information is significantly impaired, among many other ill effects.

THE IMPORTANCE OF REPETITION

Practice isn't just important for learning physical skills – it's important for learning in general. While you may study something and briefly remember all of the useful information afterwards, the chances are that you won't keep those memories for very long unless you take the chance a short while later to remind yourself of what you've just learned. This is called 'rehearsal'.

The more you repeat something, the better you will remember it, and what's great about this is that this happens without any special effort – just the act of refamiliarizing yourself with it should be enough. This will work to some extent no matter what you are trying to remember, although the number of rehearsals required may vary.

REPETITION TIMETABLE

After you have taken in information you wish to remember, aim to briefly review it again immediately. This will help reinforce what you have just read or seen. An overview of each area will suffice, but if you come across parts where you don't remember much at all then review those in more detail.

Rehearsal becomes more effective when repeated. So, the next day, take a look back over the same material, and refamiliarize yourself with it. There may well be parts you have forgotten about, so pay extra attention to these if you can. Then, about a week later, take the time to review it again. This third rehearsal will help really consolidate your memories.

A month later, however, you may find that your memory is starting to fade, so now is a good chance to take another look, and review whatever it is you are hoping to memorize. By rehearsing it again you are helping ensure that the memories will be strongly reinforced within your brain.

Finally, perhaps another couple of months after your last revision, you could review all of the material one more time.

REPEATING IN DIFFERENT FORMS

To help make a memory stronger, when you go back over the same material it's helpful to try presenting the content to yourself in a different way, to force yourself to think it through from a fresh angle. One option might be to find similar content from a different source, either by reading something different on the same subject or by watching a presentation that covers some of the same material.

Another method for increasing the efficiency of a later rehearsal is to try transforming the information in some way. For example, perhaps you are trying to learn a set of historical dates. The first and second times through you might just try to remember the events and their dates. But when you later come to review it, this time try picturing the event and finding a way to weave the date into the picture, so for example if it's a long-ago battle you could have a knight holding up a shield with the date of the battle on it. The aim is to look for a different way of remembering the fact, and what's more the repetition does more than just reinforce the existing memory but also provides a new way for you to later be able to retrieve the memorized fact.

An alternative method is to simply rephrase the information you are learning. If it is a list of facts, try expressing them differently, even just by reversing the sentences in some way. So instead of 'King John was born in 1166,' you could reorder it as you read it to 'In 1166, King John was born.' Just this simple act helps stop you simply glossing over the information.

REPETITION MEMORY EXERCISES

16. Read this phrase five times, then put the book down and do something else for a minute. After a minute, see how accurately you can recall it. Then read it a few more times, and try again five minutes later.

Incongruous infill injects inane intersections into institutions – it's insane!

17. Using the repetition method described on the preceding pages, learn as many of these historical dates as possible. Five minutes after you are done, use the test on the opposite page to see how many you remember.

1789	George Washington elected first US President
1797	John Adams succeeds him as President
1801	Thomas Jefferson becomes third US President
1826	John Adams and Thomas Jefferson both die independently on July 4th
1861	Abraham Lincoln becomes 16th US President
1865	Abraham Lincoln assassinated at Ford's Theatre
1881	James Garfield becomes 20th US President
1901	Theodore Roosevelt becomes 25th US President
1913	William Taft becomes 27th US President
1929	Herbert Hoover becomes 31st US President

Now see how many of the following questions you can answer:

18. Who became US President in 1881?

19. Who was the 27th US President?

20. Which two successive Presidents died on the exact same day?

21. Where was Abraham Lincoln assassinated?

22. Herbert Hoover was what number US President?

Reread all of the facts, and make another effort to memorize them. Then return in an hour and see how you do with these:

23. Who was the 20th US President?

24. What was the name of the 25th US President?

25. Who did Jefferson succeed as US President?

26. In what year did Washington become US President?

27. Who was the 16th US President?

Finally, reread the content and then return tomorrow to try these:

28. Who were the first three US Presidents?

29. In what year was Abraham Lincoln assassinated?

30. In what year did William Taft become US President?

31. Who was the 31st US President?

THE IMPORTANCE OF PAYING ATTENTION

If you aren't paying attention to something, you are unlikely to remember much about it. It stands to reason, and yet it's somehow an easily forgotten fact, especially when you are feeling pressured to learn something.

This means, for example, that you shouldn't be watching TV or listening to a spoken radio programme while trying to memorize material. Your attention will be so divided that you will be essentially doing neither task well – you'd be better off skimming through the memorization task and then watching the TV show, rather than trying to do both together.

Sometimes it is difficult to pay attention, especially if we are not particularly interested in a subject. If this is the case, either try working in short sessions with regular rewards for completing a session, or look for some way of making the material more interesting to you. For example, use a video introduction, if you find it easier than reading, or vice versa. Different people prefer different styles of learning, so if for example you are reading up on a subject but finding it hard to follow, then if possible you could try reading another book on the same subject from a different author.

DISTRACTIONS

Distractions come in two forms:

1. Small distractions, which mean that we don't learn as effectively as we should. This includes for example alerts on our phones that take our attention away from what we've just been working on.

2. More significant distractions, which entirely disrupt our train of thought and shift our attention to a completely different task. Often we may then find it hard to actually switch our attention back to the original task, especially if the distraction was more 'fun' than the learning task we are meant to be engaged in.

When it comes to learning for the purposes of memorization, it's really important that you know when you *are* learning and you know when you are *not*. Pausing a task to focus on something else is fine in and of itself, but it's important that you properly pay attention to things you wish to remember. Try to remove yourself from sources of background conversation, and if you're listening to music then try to pick something that doesn't keep taking your attention – instrumental music that plays at a more or less consistent volume may be best.

You could also ask other people not to disturb you. This could be a physical 'I'm busy' sign on a door, or it could be a status change on an online service to indicate that you don't want to be disturbed.

FOCUS

'Focus' doesn't just refer to paying attention, but also to the specific area you are concentrating on at any one time. Sometimes a subject can feel overwhelmingly vast, and a scattergun approach to it may not be the best bet.

When you started to learn maths at school, you began with very basic principles and then built up from there. The same approach can work with other subjects. Focus on a particular area and devote your concentration to that one section of the subject, rather than trying to learn a little bit of everything all at once. Find the part that you find most interesting, and begin there.

Once you have built a basic foundation of knowledge about a subject, it will be easier for your brain to make sense of additional related information, and the amount of heavy lifting your brain needs to do to memorize additional facts will begin to decrease.

CONNECTING MEMORIES

One key method for making a memory more durable is to connect it to something that you already know about. An abstract memory floating on its own inside your head is unlikely to survive very long. You might for example read an entire book of world history, and then at the end of it remember almost nothing other than a few names and perhaps the odd date. You would have covered such a wide range of subjects that there would be little connection between them to make them naturally memorable. What's more, if you were reading an introductory volume of such a type then you would probably have little background knowledge to anchor your memories to. So, unless you paid special attention to the book, or it really held your attention, then you would probably forget most of its contents surprisingly quickly.

To use a memory, you need to have both learned it *and* also be able to retrieve it. Connecting a new memory into an existing memory helps with both of these – not only do you add an extra retrieval route, but the connection should make it easier to learn too.

POSSIBLE CONNECTIONS

There are so many possible relationships between things that you will be able to connect almost anything to an existing memory if you try. Say, for example, you are trying to learn that chalk is, chemically, calcium carbonate. You can perhaps think of a blackboard with white chalk marks on it, and then remember the white marks you get in a kettle from hard water, which are calcium deposits. Immediately you have used 'white mark' to connect 'chalk' to 'calcium', and then from there you could think about the kettle bubbling, which is like carbonated water bubbling in a fizzy drink. So you have created a connection between the memory of the word 'chalk' and its chemical name, 'calcium carbonate'. This makes it much more memorable than just trying to remember the abstract fact on its own. Look for things you already know, and see if you can connect them – it doesn't matter if the connection is ridiculous, since the point is to make it memorable.

ASSOCIATION

Being able to retrieve a memory is a key part of using it, since without a way of accessing the memory it isn't of any use. This hints as to the mechanism by which memories are stored, which is that they are associated with one another. No memory exists entirely independently of another. A memory of a childhood party is connected to other memories of family, and even a memory, such as that event 'X' happened on date 'Y', connects both X to Y and then Y back to X. In practice, the connections and associations between memories can be extremely rich and intricate.

The richer and stronger those associations are, the better able we are to store and retrieve a memory. Think of anything you like, and ask yourself what you associate it with. Consider the Sun – it provides heat, light, and the pattern of night and day; then your thoughts might go on to the fact it is a star, produces sun spots, and so on. Or think about a dog. You probably don't think of dogs in terms of their precise descriptions – 'a domesticated carnivorous mammal that typically has a long snout, an acute sense of smell, non-retractile claws, and a barking, howling, or whining voice', to quote the Oxford Dictionary of English. Instead you perhaps think of actual dogs you know or have known, or of breeds of dog, or even about pets in general. There is a web of associated thoughts that trigger, and even if you don't care for dogs at all you could still probably carry on writing down these associations for many minutes.

Connecting memories to other memories and knowledge is key to remembering them. The more you can think about how a particular fact or thing you wish to remember connects to other things you know of, the stronger that memory should be.

MEMORY ASSOCIATIONS

32. To help demonstrate just how powerful memory associations can be, make a list of as many things connected with the word 'cat' as you can. Continue on another sheet of paper if you need to.

_____

_____

_____

_____

_____

_____

33. Now try to create as many possible connections as you can between the following two words – they can be as ridiculous as you like:

Honesty   Coffee

_____

_____

_____

_____

34. Create associations to help you memorize this fact:

The chance of a clover having four leaves is 1 in 10,000.

Write down the first three words that come to mind for each of the following:

35. The Internet _____ _____ _____

36. Maturity _____ _____ _____

37. Dentists _____ _____ _____

38. An orchestra _____ _____ _____

39. Lotteries _____ _____ _____

40. A giraffe _____ _____ _____

41. Find a sticky note and cover over all but the last of the columns above, so you can only see the third word you thought of. Come back tomorrow and see if you can still remember which item triggered that word. Then, for any you are stuck on, reveal the second word and see if that helps you remember. And finally reveal the first word too, if needed. How much prompting did you require?

42. By finding associations between the items, even if they are ridiculous, see if you can remember the items in this list after five minutes has passed. If you need prompting on the first item it's okay to peek, but see how well you can do on the rest without any help.

Doughnut	Toothpaste	Milk
Suncream	Cough medicine	Kitchen towel
Scarf	Umbrella	Footpath

43. Finally, without checking back, what is the likelihood of any given clover having four leaves?

TAKING NOTE OF MEMORIES

As we have seen, effective learning requires paying attention and then rehearsing what you have learned. But going over facts again and again can be time-consuming, which risks you attempting to do it so quickly that it becomes ineffective. What you ideally need are some good notes, which will summarize what you have learned and help you go back over it quickly – as well as present it in a different format, which will also assist in making it more memorable.

The simple act of taking notes on something is a first act of repetition. Whether you highlight, underline or write down the material, you are forced to go over it at least once – the first time to absorb it, and the second time to write it down. In reducing it to note form you are also requiring yourself to apply a certain amount of attention and thought, both of which assist in forming a stronger memory.

It is good to organize notes into sections, rather than make them a long rambling series of handwritten scribbles, or a stream-of-consciousness-style typed document, for example. If you don't have time to do this as you go, perhaps because you are following along with a live presentation, then you should make the time to do so afterwards while they are still fresh in your mind – and what's more, this can then be your third time reviewing the material. Even if you don't need to organize the material, you can still edit and tidy up your notes.

When you come to revise the material later, you then have organized records which mean that you can both quickly orient yourself to the relevant section of the material *and* more easily break it up into sections. This can make it easier to concentrate, or to split your revision over multiple sessions if necessary. And, by having the reduced notes in the first place, you are able to go through the material far more quickly than simply revisiting the original longer-form content.

It could even be beneficial to make further notes based on your own notes, clarifying any sections you found hard to follow or remember – which may also require some additional research, if there is information actually missing from your notes.

DICTATED NOTES

Some people like to dictate notes, where practical, and the act of transferring between different media can actually help make them more memorable. If you read a piece of text, dictate a summary, then transcribe and further summarize that summary into written notes, for example, you may do a better job of memorizing it effortlessly than if you had simply kept it in written form the entire time. Or this might not help you at all – it depends on many factors, including of course your ability to summarize notes orally as well as in writing. It is, however, always worth experimenting to see if there is a particular procedure that works well for you.

ANSWERING QUESTIONS

A good way to check you have learned your notes is to have a friend or colleague question you on them. You can always return the favour at a later date. Anything you are unable to answer will aid you in identifying weaknesses in your knowledge to focus on. The process also works as an additional rehearsal of the information, so even if you do well being quizzed you're still helping yourself to remember the information.

READ OUT YOUR NOTES

Simply repeating your notes in another form, by converting the written text into spoken words, also in and of itself can help you memorize them. This can force you to focus on them much better than simply silently reading them.

NOTE-TAKING EXERCISES

44. Take notes on the following passage, using your chosen method:

Word ladder puzzles were popularized in the late 19th century by Lewis Carroll, author of *Alice's Adventures in Wonderland*. He is well known as a writer, but he was also an accomplished mathematician and was very interested in logic and puzzles. On top of this, he was also an Anglican deacon, and a successful photographer.

Although he wrote as Lewis Carroll, his real name was Charles Lutwidge Dodgson. He wrote further fantastical fiction in *Through the Looking-Glass*, in which Alice returned, as well as in his poems, which include *The Hunting of the Snark* and *Jabberwocky*.

He wrote almost 100,000 letters throughout his life, according to a register he kept of his correspondence. He even wrote a guide to writing letters, called *Eight or Nine Wise Words About Letter-Writing*.

He died in 1898 of pneumonia, at his sister's home in Guildford, just two weeks shy of his 66th birthday.

45. Using your notes, review what you have just read and if appropriate summarize and tidy your notes.

46. Reread the original passage and see if there is anything you have missed out of your notes. Add to your notes if necessary. Then take a break and come back to the next page after at least an hour has passed.

Answer the following questions:

47. How old was Lewis Carroll when he died?

48. What was the name of his guide to writing letters?

49. Name two of his poems.

50. And name two of his books.

51. What was his real name?

52. Apart from his renown as a writer, list five other activities he was noted for.

53. Around how many letters did he write in his life?

54. What type of puzzle does the article say he popularized?

55. Where was he when he died, and what did he die of?

56. Create your own note-taking exercises. Find an article of interest to you, such as a feature article from a newspaper or an extended item of writing you find online, and summarize its key points. There is no need to note down *everything* it covers. Then write yourself five questions and answers on what you have just read, and come back in an hour to see if you can still answer them.

57. Now reread your notes, and the article too if necessary, and write yourself five more questions – make sure they are on the parts you had the most trouble remembering. Come back to all of your questions tomorrow, and see how you do on them.

ACRONYMS

Acronyms form the basis of a simple, but effective, memory technique. An acronym is a sequence of words that is condensed into just the initials of those words, and then used as a single word, as in for example 'CD' for 'compact disc'. The definition of an acronym is also often extended to include any abbreviation derived from the letters also *within* various words. For example, 'Interpol' for '**Inter**national Criminal **Pol**ice Organization'.

You need to take the time to form them in the first place, but once formed they can be remarkably memorable. For example, it is typically much easier to remember the order and colours of the rainbow by recalling the acronym 'ROYGBIV' (with the initials standing for **r**ed, **o**range, **y**ellow, **g**reen, **b**lue, **i**ndigo and **v**iolet) – which perhaps seems counter-intuitive, given that this particular acronym is not particularly easy to pronounce. The fact that it works anyway just goes to show the power of acronyms.

Acronyms are a good memory technique because they allow you to:

- compress a series of information into a single item,

- remember the exact order of information,

- and provide a trigger for you to recall information you already know, given that the first letter of a word is often particularly helpful.

BUILDING ACRONYMS

If an existing acronym isn't lying around waiting to be used, then you will need to make your own. Let's say, for example, that you want to remember the four bases in a DNA molecule. These are adenine, guanine, cytosine and thymine. Given those initials, and no need to remember them in any particular order, we could come up for example with CAT-G – perhaps a reference to the unique gravity that allows cats to always land on their feet (or so it is claimed...).

If you are already familiar with the DNA bases, then quite possibly all you will need to recall them is something to *prompt* you of the four, so this acronym alone will be entirely sufficient. But acronyms work best when reminding us of terms we already know, yet can't easily recall. They won't help so much with recalling things we are unfamiliar with. If, for example, you have never come across the bases before, then by now you may have forgotten what they stand for. See if you can complete them right away, without looking back:

C_____ A_____ T_____ G_____

PRONOUNCEABLE ACRONYMS

The most memorable acronyms are easy to pronounce, which you can facilitate by inserting some extra letters as you please. You will then hopefully remember that you have done this and not end up getting too confused!

Say, for example, that you want to remember the first five elements in the periodic table. They are hydrogen, helium, lithium, beryllium and boron. A straight acronym in this case, HHLBB, may be of limited use since it is not especially memorable. We could try taking the first two letters, but even 'hy he li be bo' is not brilliant. What we can do instead, therefore, is insert arbitrary letters – so long as we do this consistently it won't cause any problems. For example, '**Hi**, **hell baby**!' is much easier to remember – we can pronounce it, and it's even something we could visualize too. When we use it, we simply ignore every other letter. Similarly, with sufficient time we can build acronyms to make many things in life more memorable, and what's more the technique also helps us to remember the order things come in.

ACRONYM ACTIVITIES

Start by making up for yourself what the following acronyms *might* stand for. There are no correct answers here!

58. D F D R   – in the field of hairdressing

59. E P R   – in the field of swimming

60. S R P S   – in the field of fashion

61. P P L N   – in the field of politics

62. I L M R   – in a field of your choice, and similarly for those below

63. R R S

64. P R G I S L

65. N N N N N

Now use the acronym method to remember these facts about elements in the periodic table and their chemical symbols:

66. Ag = Silver   Au = Gold

67. He = Helium   Ne = Neon

68. Use acronyms to remember elements 6 to 9 in the periodic table:

6 = C = Carbon

7 = N = Nitrogen

8 = O = Oxygen

9 = F = Fluorine

Come up with your own pronounceable acronyms for these sequences:

69. Mercury, Venus, Earth, Mars, Jupiter, Saturn, Uranus, Neptune

70. January, February, March, April, May, June

71. Monday, Tuesday, Wednesday, Thursday, Friday

72. You can also try using the acronym method to remember the locations of successive Summer Olympics:

1900	Paris
1904	St Louis
1908	London
1912	Stockholm
1916	*Cancelled due to World War I*
1920	Antwerp
1924	Paris

73. Test out how well your acronym for the Summer Olympics locations works by now filling in the locations in the empty table below:

1900	_____
1904	_____
1908	_____
1912	_____
1916	_____
1920	_____
1924	_____

ACROSTICS

Acronyms are a powerful technique, but they can be hard to create. They are best for remembering short sequences of information. So what if we want to remember much longer sets of facts, such as say the names of British monarchs in order? From 1707 (when the first Act of Union became law), we have Anne, George, George, George, George, William, Victoria, Edward, George, Edward, George, Elizabeth. Good luck finding a memorable acronym for AGGGGWVEGEGE!

Longer sequences such as this are where acrostics can come in. Instead of looking for a single word, we look for a memorable sentence or phrase which can link the initials together. For example, to remember the order of the planets, with initials MVEMJSUN, we could say '**m**y **v**aluable **e**arrings **m**ake **j**ewels **s**hine **u**ntil **n**oon', or something equally strange and yet hopefully memorable. This single phrase is easier to remember than the order of the planets as a discrete set of facts. Although acrostics are longer than acronyms, often remembering just the start of an acrostic will trigger the memory of the rest with relative ease.

With the list of British monarchs the challenge is greater. We could perhaps have '**a** **g**ood **g**iant **g**ave **G**eorge, **w**ith **v**egetables, **e**very **g**lorious **e**vening **g**ala, **e**vermore'. This may not be entirely brilliant, but it's best to quickly form a complete acrostic and then refine it, rather than agonize over perfecting it in a single go.

FLEXIBLE ACROSTICS

With acronyms we allowed ourselves some flexibility to make them more memorable. With acrostics we can do just the same, *so long as* we remember the rules we make for ourselves! For example, it would be a good idea to allow articles and prepositions (the, a, from, to, etc) to be included without requiring them to stand for anything in the acrostic. So long as we decide to always apply this rule, we can use them without any trouble since we will know to ignore them. An alternative option would be to decide that any word of three or fewer letters should be ignored.

If we ignore words under three letters, for example, we can now remember our British monarchs with '**A**fter **g**iving **G**eorge a **g**reat **g**ift, **W**illiam **v**anquished **e**very **g**iant in **e**ach **g**arden of England'. The more absurd you can make it, the better, since you will then find it easier to recall.

PASSWORDS

No doubt you have countless passwords for equally countless online services, and yet we are told to never write them down and *never* to repeat them! Not repeating them is a good idea, since otherwise if one service is compromised then all of your accounts with the same login details are too. But how can you remember lots of passwords?

One method is to use acrostics. These can even be based on the site. Say, for example, you shop at Amazon. You could come up with something memorable that uses the site's name. For example, 'The Amazon river makes me shiver' gives you six letters, 'TArmms', that are not a common password string. On top of that you could add on a regular password that you *do* use across multiple sites, in order to make a sufficiently long password. Say, for example, you regularly use 'eggplant22' as a password, your Amazon password would then be 'TArmmseggplant22'. Now *that* is a secure password!

You can therefore combine two tactics – a shared password with a small additional change for each site so it isn't repeated – with an acrostic to make that customization completely private to you. Even if you write it down, you are still reasonably secure because it would not be obvious to anyone else what it is (so long as you don't label it with the site name), or how to combine it with your separately memorized general password.

ACROSTIC EXERCISES

For each of the following sets of facts, come up with an acrostic to help you remember it:

74. The Famous Five are Julian, Dick, Anne, Georgina and Timmy

75. The Secret Seven are Peter, Janet, Jack, Barbara, George, Pam and Colin

76. The first six Mr. Men are Mr. Tickle, Mr. Greedy, Mr. Happy, Mr. Nosey, Mr. Sneeze and Mr. Bump

77. This one is particularly tricky and may require you to acronym multiple letters from the names:
The Borrowers are Arrietty, Pod, Homily, Hendreary, Lupy and Eggletina

Here are some acrostics for very common sequences. Can you work out what they represent?

78. So sue my totally weird third finger!

79. Just forever may all my jumpers jump away

80. Only the tame flea flew so slowly

81. Really only young giraffes breed if vacationing

82. See if you can come up with an acronym to help you remember the first five British Prime Ministers of the 20th century:

    Salisbury, Balfour, Campbell-Bannerman, Asquith, Lloyd George

83. Now try using the acronym of British Prime Ministers to recall them all in the correct order.

84. Without looking back, who were the first six Mr. Men?

85. Who were the Famous Five?

86. Who were the Secret Seven?

87. Who were the six Borrowers?

88. And again without looking back, who were the first five British Prime Ministers of the twentieth century?

89. Now create some acronyms with any letters of your choice, making them as memorable as possible, so you could use them as ready-to-go password components in the future. Try to make them of varying length, so ideally some five, six, seven and eight-letter ones:

RELATED FACTS

We have already seen that memories are stronger when associated with existing memories, and in a similar way facts also become more memorable when learned in context.

Say, for example, that you wanted to remember that the capital of Mali is Bamako. On its own, you might find it hard to recall, especially if you are trying to remember a long list of countries and capitals. But if you learn a little about Mali, or Bamako, it suddenly gets a lot easier. For example, Bamako comes from a word in the local Bambara language that means 'crocodile tail', and is situated on the Niger river, which is the principal river in western Africa. Now we have a few facts to remember together about Mali and Bamako, and remembering this small cluster of information is easier than just remembering the relatively abstract fact that there is a country Mali with capital city Bamako. Knowing this extra information can also provide us with other ways to retrieve these details from our memory.

CONTRASTING RELATED FACTS
A useful technique when learning facts is to contrast them in some way. For example, instead of – or in addition to – learning the information above about Bamako, you could also contrast Mali and its capital with other capital cities and countries in western Africa. For example, by some estimates Bamako is the sixth-fastest growing city in the world, and the fastest growing city in Africa, both of which may be interesting enough to be memorable in their own right. You can then contrast this with the other cities that are growing faster – it is for example one step above Lagos, a city in Nigeria which is the seventh-fastest growing city in the world. And you can even then go on to learn further information, such as that the capital of Nigeria is the recently built planned city of Abuja.

RELATED FACT EXERCISES

90. There are 18 countries in western Africa. For each of them, write down just their capital cities first, and try to memorize these without any additional help:

Country	Capital City
Benin	
Burkina Faso	
Cape Verde (an island)	
Gambia	
Ghana	
Guinea	
Guinea-Bissau	
Ivory Coast	
Liberia	
Mali	
Mauritania	
Niger	
Nigeria	
Saint Helena (an island)	
Senegal	
Sierra Leone	
São Tomé and Príncipe	
Togo	

91. If you have already completed the previous puzzle, use the repeated list of countries below to see how well you can *recall* the capital cities. Then, for any you did not remember, or found hard to recall, find some interesting facts about the cities and add them below:

Country	Capital City and Interesting Facts
Benin	
Burkina Faso	
Cape Verde (an island)	
Gambia	
Ghana	
Guinea	
Guinea-Bissau	
Ivory Coast	
Liberia	
Mali	
Mauritania	
Niger	
Nigeria	
Saint Helena (an island)	
Senegal	
Sierra Leone	
São Tomé and Príncipe	
Togo	

92. Now come back to this page tomorrow, and see how many of the capital cities you can *now* recall from their countries:

Country	Capital City
Benin	_____
Burkina Faso	_____
Cape Verde (an island)	_____
Gambia	_____
Ghana	_____
Guinea	_____
Guinea-Bissau	_____
Ivory Coast	_____
Liberia	_____
Mali	_____
Mauritania	_____
Niger	_____
Nigeria	_____
Saint Helena (an island)	_____
Senegal	_____
Sierra Leone	_____
São Tomé and Príncipe	_____
Togo	_____

CHUNKING MEMORY

The acronym and acrostic memory techniques discussed in the previous chapter work by combining multiple pieces of information into a single item. Even though these combined facts are more complex than any one individual item, the overall effort of memorization is substantially eased by combining them together in a memorable way.

The same technique can be used at a more basic level, to bind sequential digits or words into groups and then memorize them as if a single item. This technique is called 'chunking'.

CREATING CHUNKS

You will naturally chunk some information already. For example, if you see the year 2017 then you will not think of it as two, zero, one, seven, but rather as twenty seventeen, or maybe two thousand and seventeen. Similarly, you might think of the author C. S. Lewis as 'CS' 'Lewis'. In other words, if you remember the 'C', you will also remember the 'S', because you have joined them into a single item in your memory.

Telephone numbers are also usually both written and pronounced in chunks. It's both easier to follow *and* memorize a number written like this:

+44 1234 987 456

...rather than as a single string of digits:

+441234987456

SIZES OF CHUNKS

How many items can you fit into a chunk? A good number to aim for is two to six items. Beyond that you may need to create multiple chunks, and link them together or associate them in some other way. Interestingly, once you have fitted everything into your chunk, it does seem to then act as a single item for the purposes of your short-term memory storage (see page 17).

The precise number of items you can fit into a chunk depends on how complex those items are. In addition, you won't be able to combine multiple chunks into a single chunk until such time as the individual chunks are memorized in and of themselves.

CHUNK COMPONENTS

As with acrostics, your chunks of information don't need to be made up purely of the content you specifically wish to learn. You can combine them with anything that makes them more memorable, whether that's a rhyme, a joke, a reference to a person or place, or even a visual connection. For example, if you are trying to remember the British postcode 'GU11 5EA', if you observe that it looks like 'gull sea', you have essentially combined the entire postcode into a single, far more easily memorable chunk. The way you form the chunks is entirely up to you.

PRE-BUILT CHUNKS

Many advanced memorization techniques are based on pre-chunking information that is likely to be encountered. This means that in advance of attempting to memorize content we learn a specific system for reducing the complexity of that content. For example, if we are trying to remember the order of a deck of cards, we could pre-learn a single word or person for every individual card – and then instead of having to remember *both* '4' and 'spades', we'd only remember 'fork', because in advance we have chunked '4' and 'spades' into the word 'fork'.

Pre-built chunks can also be used for more day-to-day memorization requirements, such as remembering your hotel room, a friend's phone number, a PIN or even a password.

CHUNKING EXERCISES

For each of the following, experiment with chunking them in order to make them more memorable:

93. WC2B 5EX

94. 07931 583308

95. 198 919 901 991

96. Llanfairpwllgwyngyll

97. Pneumonoultramicroscopicsilicovolcanoconiosis

98. Did you spot the hidden sequence in the 12-digit number above? It would have made it much easier if you did!

Use the chunking method to remember each of the following words. Experiment with breaking them down in different ways:

99.   Honorificabilitudinitatibus

_____

_____

100.   Floccinaucinihilipilification

_____

_____

101.   Pseudopseudohypoparathyroidism

_____

_____

Cover over the three words you were given to chunk above, and see if you can write each one down in full. How much of each word can you recall correctly?

102. What was the first word, starting 'Honor...'?

_____

103. What was the second word, starting 'Flocc...'?

_____

104. What was the third word, starting 'Pseud...'?

_____

VISUALIZATION OF MEMORIES

Using visualization to help you store a memory is a useful technique for finding an alternative, hopefully more memorable, way of storing information inside your brain. It doesn't mean that you need to be able to actually draw or in some other way make visual images in the real world, nor that you must be able to accurately picture items and describe exactly what they look like. But what it does mean is that you can use a visual concept to represent a memory, or a chunk of items that you wish to remember. This has two potential benefits:

- You are storing the memory in an extra way, which means you have another way of recalling it;

- You are hopefully describing it in an intrinsically more *memorable* way, especially if the visualization is applied to relatively dry facts.

SIMPLE VISUALIZATION

When there is a readily available visual image for something you are trying to remember, it can really help just to quickly think of it as you memorize the fact. For example, say you are learning that polar bears live in the Arctic, not the Antarctic, you could quickly picture a polar bear sitting contentedly on top of the world – and bingo, that memory probably isn't going away! You don't need to accurately visualize a polar bear; you can for example imagine a white cartoon bear sitting proudly on a ridiculously small globe. The point is that the image helps you remember the fact, not that the image is so detailed you get distracted building the image.

ADVANCED VISUALIZATION

Not all information lends itself to immediate visualization, but by connecting to associated concepts you can usually find a way. Consider, perhaps, a desire to learn the names of the five most populous states in the United States. These are, in decreasing order of population, California, Texas, Florida, New York and Illinois.

First up, are there any immediate images that spring to mind? For example, you might think of alligators when you think of Florida, or of the Golden Gate Bridge when you think of California. Maybe Texas makes you think of a cowboy hat. So you could remember the first three, in order, by imagining looking at the Golden Gate Bridge when all of a sudden a cowboy hat floats under, hotly pursued by an alligator. You can build up images, and even visual stories, that are as complex as you like. And, as always, making them a bit absurd helps make them more memorable. But if you go *too* far down that path, you may find that they become so ridiculously unlikely that you can no longer remember them!

ABSTRACT VISUALIZATION

Visualization of memories doesn't have to involve literal images. It can also include other perceptions too. For example, if trying to remember the elder of a pair of brothers, you could remember that they were born in alphabetical order – or conversely that they were *not* born in alphabetical order. You would in other words visualize the order of the words, and 'see' them in a particular order – alphabetical, or reverse alphabetical – and then use this to help you remember the information about who was the eldest. You could even attach further concepts to help you remember – for example, you might consider that alphabetical order is 'correct order', and therefore you could remember that the brothers were born in the 'correct' or conversely the 'incorrect' order. Not a concept to explain to their parents out loud, perhaps, but it would probably help you remember. Your exact visualization is only useful for you to know.

Other methods for visualizing orders include looking at the length of words, or connecting them to some other ordered sequence you are already familiar with, and remembering what differs – if anything.

VISUALIZATION EXERCISES

105. Try visualizing an ordinary household object, such as maybe a sofa you have in a living room. Can you see it in your mind, without actually looking at it? What colour is it? How many cushions does it have? What does each cushion look like? Does it have legs? Then look at the actual item and see if there is anything you can describe that you missed.

Initial notes

_____

_____

Further observations

_____

_____

106. Now pick something more complex, such as the outside of a house or building you are familiar with. Describe this as precisely as you can, just from memory – then, if you can, check against reality.

_____

_____

_____

_____

_____

_____

_____

107. Use a visual memory method to remember the following chain of animals, in the order they are given here:

Crocodile	Aardvark	Marmot
Red panda	Seal	Badger
Armadillo	Weasel	Guinea pig
Echidna	Elephant	Bushbaby

108. See if you can memorize this sequence of Winter Olympic host countries, from 1980 through to 2014, by using a visual memory method to link the countries:

United States	Yugoslavia
Canada	France
Norway	Japan
United States	Italy
Canada	Russia

109. Now cover the top of this page and test yourself on the 16 animals. Starting with the given first animal, see how many you can recall:

Crocodile _____

_____

_____

_____

POETRY AND SOUND

Rhyming phrases are often extremely memorable, which is one reason why poems are much easier to learn than general prose. The metric rhythm of a poem is also important too, since the rhythm naturally cues you into how many words you are looking for, and the likely sentence structure. Combine the two and you have a powerful built-in aide-memoire that makes poetry a powerful learning technique.

What's more, the natural restrictions inherent in writing a poem, of having to find words that rhyme and fit to the metre, means that each word may well have been especially carefully chosen. The use of vivid, expressive language also helps make them even more memorable. Further still, the words may even have been chosen to fit with both their semantic meaning and also their sound too, further reinforcing their usage.

Is it any wonder, then, that the sagas that were long passed down through oral tradition were written in poetic form? Consider for example Homer's epic poems, the *Iliad* and the *Odyssey*, or that most playwrights once exclusively wrote in verse.

Perhaps you still remember a poem you heard long ago, or at least parts of it, or limericks and rhymes you maybe last recited as a small child. It's not hard to believe, therefore, that this is a good technique for memorizing material.

USING A POEM TO RETAIN KNOWLEDGE
Earlier in the book we used the British monarchs as an example for memorization, and there is a particular poem that was once taught to generations of British schoolchildren to help them learn the history of the monarchy – it is no longer taught, however, since children are no

longer expected to learn such things. And while it is probably of no use to most people to be able to know the line of former royalty, the general techniques of memorization have been widely lost along with the perhaps unnecessary knowledge that accompanied them. The part that covered the first half of the twentieth century read as follows:

> *Edward seven next, and then*
> *George the fifth in 1910;*
> *Ted the eighth soon abdicated*
> *Then George the sixth was coronated*

It may not be a work of high art, but the rhymes not only help you remember the basic progression – Edward VII, George V, Edward VIII and then George VI – but also give you some extra facts, such as that Edward VIII abdicated and that George V came to the throne in 1910.

With a relatively small amount of effort, you can also devise rhymes that help you remember all kinds of material. And, of course, poems are recited in a specific order, so as in the example above you can use them to remember sequences too.

MUSIC AND SOUNDS

We don't usually consciously remember specific sounds we hear, perhaps because we rarely have any need to recall any particular noise. We do, however, remember songs and tunes, often very accurately and with both minimal exposure and effort. And what is a song, but a poem with additional music? So perhaps the holy grail of memorization is to not only come up with a poem, but to also fit it to a song. In fact, the excerpt for remembering the royals above was designed to be sung to the tune of the Christmas carol *Good King Wenceslas*. Give it a go yourself, and see if you can make it work – it just about fits!

One time when we do focus on specific sounds is when listening to voices. Some people are able to mimic a person's accent, diction and other audible characteristics from even just a brief sample – which suggest our memory for these things is rather powerful!

POETIC MEMORY EXERCISES

Create simple rhyming couplets to help memorize these facts:

110. Marie Curie won the Nobel Prize for Physics in 1903

_____

_____

111. Robert Koch won the Nobel Prize for Medicine in 1905

_____

_____

112. Otto Hahn won the Nobel Prize for Chemistry in 1944

_____

_____

113. Ernest Hemingway won the Nobel Prize for Literature in 1954

_____

_____

114. Norman Borlaug won the Nobel Peace Prize in 1970

_____

_____

115. Write a poem to learn the following set of statistics. Can you use the repetition of the winners to help with the memorization?

Wimbledon Singles Champions

Year	Gentlemen's Singles	Ladies' Singles
1980	Björn Borg	Evonne Cawley
1981	John McEnroe	Chris Evert
1982	Jimmy Connors	Martina Navratilova
1983	John McEnroe	Martina Navratilova
1984	John McEnroe	Martina Navratilova
1985	Boris Becker	Martina Navratilova
1986	Boris Becker	Martina Navratilova

116. Now write a *song* to learn the following list of US states and their corresponding state flower. Set it to the tune of a Christmas carol of your choice!

US State	State Flower
Alaska	Forget-me-not
Arkansas	Apple blossom
Connecticut	Mountain laurel
Delaware	Peach blossom
Illinois	Violet
Kansas	Sunflower
Massachusetts	Mayflower
New York	Rose

BASIC NUMBER MEMORIZATION

From time to time we all need to remember numbers. Perhaps we no longer need to learn phone numbers, but you might still need to recall for example the room numbers of colleagues in a hotel, a price you have just been quoted over the phone, the departure time and gate of a flight, the date of a birthday or indeed countless other number-based pieces of information. So how do we go about this?

CONNECTING TO OTHER NUMBERS

The easiest way to remember a number, as something other than a string of digits, is simply to connect it to something we already know of that shares the same number. Say for example we are given the number 1,969 to remember, we could consider it to be the year 1969 and then represent it by the Moon, since we know that 1969 is the year that mankind first landed on the Moon. Or we might know that it is the year Richard Nixon became President of the United States, and use the image of him instead.

This works for many numbers, but of course not all. For those numbers, and especially longer numbers, we need additional techniques.

CHUNKING NUMBERS

We covered the basic principle of breaking numbers up into chunks, so we have fewer items to remember, on page 52. But instead of simply breaking into convenient-length segments, we can try to break them up into segments that are themselves memorable by being associated with other things that we know already.

For example, the number 764,913,180 could be broken down as follows:

- 76 – which might remind us of 'Seventy Six Trombones' in the musical play *The Music Man*;

- 49 – a reference to the 'forty-niners' in the 1849 California Gold Rush;

- 13 – something unlucky, perhaps;

- 180 – doing a U-turn, i.e. of 180 degrees.

So now we can remember our number by imagining trombones being played by gold miners, who are unlucky in not finding gold and so turn around and go back home. This small, visual story is much easier to remember than the entirely abstract number, and what's more we probably only need to think 'trombone' to be able to recall all of the rest, since we chained the different parts of the story together.

Summarizing this, we first of all chunked the number. We then associated each of those chunks with an existing concept that represented that number. And then we associated the chunks with each other in sequence, so we could remember the number in order. In the process we turned it first from ten digits into four chunks, and then from four chunks into a single sequence. We can now just remember 'trombone' to recall the whole number as one single item.

NUMBERS TO PHRASES

Another method to convert a number into a different form is simply to look for words with a length that match each digit in the number, in a sentence or phrase that combines them. For example, say we have the number 2,953,446,434, we just need to find a sentence with words of that length. So for example we could have 'If Beethoven makes you bark, does Mozart help you park?'. The number of characters in each word corresponds to each digit in turn. Of course, the smarter and more memorable the phrase is, the easier the number will be to remember.

NUMBER MEMORIZATION

Use the methods on the previous two pages to try to memorize each of these individual numbers:

117. 386,873

118. 7,385,942

119. 93,868,738

120. 993,838,583

121. 101,001,001

122. 2,021,020,121

123. 9,769,769,769,679

124. 3,563,653,563,653

125. 18,572,058,290,285,092

Now try using a similar method as part of your technique for memorizing the following numbers plus their meanings:

126. Pi = 3.141592654

127. e = 2.718281828

128. Phi = 1.618033988

129. Speed of sound at sea level = 340.29 metres/second

130. Speed of light = 299,792,458 metres/second

131. Try learning the decimal values of each of the following fractions, using a number memorization method:

1/1	=	1
1/2	=	0.5
1/3	=	0.333333333
1/4	=	0.25
1/5	=	0.2
1/6	=	0.166666667
1/7	=	0.142857143
1/8	=	0.125
1/9	=	0.111111111
1/10	=	0.1
1/11	=	0.090909091
1/12	=	0.083333333
1/13	=	0.076923077
1/14	=	0.071428571
1/15	=	0.066666667

REMEMBERING NAMES AND FACES

Have you ever been in the embarrassing situation where somebody knows who you are, but you have no idea who they are? Or conversely, have you ever bumped into someone you've seen on a stage, TV show or elsewhere and thought you knew them, only to realize after saying hello that they have never met you before?

The human brain is incredibly good at spotting faces. So good, in fact, that it sees them everywhere – in the Moon, in a shadow on the wall, in the holes on a piece of cheese, and even in a trivially simple emoticon:

:)

If you can recognize a colon and a bracket as a face, you can certainly learn to more easily recognize the real human faces you are exposed to.

DESCRIBE THE FACE

It may seem obvious, given that we all have names, but attaching words to faces is a key step. We need to label that face, and attach concepts to it that we can use to help retrieve the person's details at a later date. The problem with a name on its own is that it generally does not describe the person at all, so there is no intrinsic connection between the two concepts. We need to make one, so that we can remember who they are and what their name is.

Study the person's face for just a moment. Staring is probably not wise, unless you're looking at a photo, but the chances are that you spot some distinguishing feature right away – even if that distinguishing feature is that they are unusually perfect-looking. What does their nose look like? Or what about their cheeks, the shape of their face, their eyes, their mouth, and so on? Is there something you spot about them that you could imagine being caricatured, perhaps? Does the face remind you of someone you know already, or someone you are familiar with from the media?

Once you have your identifying features, see if you can connect words for those features to the person's name. Sometimes this is easier than other times. For example, if their name is Jack Sparrow and they have a hooked nose like a bird, this will help you remember their surname; and if they look a bit like the Jack of Spades, even better!

If the person's name has no specific meaning to you, such as say 'Dave Edwards', then see what you can find in terms of associations. Does the name 'Dave' remind you of anything in and of itself? Maybe you know a Dave who is a builder, and if this person clearly spends a lot of time in the gym then could you connect them with the thought that they are a *body* builder, using the word 'builder' to link the two Daves? Or do they look really sleepy, maybe, and you can turn their surname into 'bedwards', as in that they look like they're going to bed, and remember them that way?

You can also use your other existing memory techniques to make names you are not already familiar with become more memorable, in and of themselves.

PUT THEM IN THEIR PLACE

Another tactic for remembering people is to think about where you might encounter them. This doesn't necessarily mean in actual life, but rather in the fantasy version you create to help remember them. Say for example that the person you have just met looks, for whatever reason, like they might be a stamp collector. You could then imagine them at a post office, buying stamps. Now think of someone who shares the first name of this person, and imagine *them* buying stamps. Now when you see the original person again, you might think 'post office', 'buying stamps', the person you already know of, and then therefore the actual person's name.

A MEMORY FOR FACES

132. Learn the names of each of these people:

Douglas   Kimmy   Samuel

Jemima   Victor   Chloe

133. Now cover the top half of the page, wait a minute, and see if you can name the following three people:

134. Without checking the opposite page, which of the people do these faces *most closely resemble*?

135. Look at this arrangement of simplified faces, then cover them over and see how accurately you can redraw them in the empty circles below.

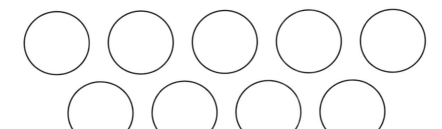

REMEMBERING PASSAGES OF TEXT

Sometimes in life we need to give a presentation, deliver a memorized sales pitch, or perform some other feat of textual recall. We might even want to recite a poem or perhaps even act on stage. In all these cases we need a good technique for learning passages of text.

If you are recalling a poem, or the script of a play, you will no doubt wish to get it word perfect. Many times, however, you will only need to remember your opening remarks, the actual points you want to make, and the order you want to make them in, and perhaps a rehearsed closing couple of sentences designed to deliver a memorable ending. Even so, you may still wish to learn a presentation or speech in an essentially verbatim style. The downside to this tactic, of course, is that if you rely on a verbatim recall and then lose your place, or forget something, you may be far more lost than if you had merely memorized a sequence of notes that you could improvise around. In practice, however, even if you intend to only learn a set of notes, the very act of practising a presentation will typically ingrain certain phrases into your presentation that you will then later repeat verbatim.

BREAKING INTO SECTIONS

When delivering a speech or presentation, there will be certain key points you don't want to ever omit. You therefore need to first break it down into those points, or basic sections, whether you intend to then deliver those sections verbatim as learned or not. This also means you can break your practice and learning down by section too, rather than trying to memorize an entire length of text as a single passage.

Once you have split your talk into sections, you will need a technique to prompt you for each section, so you can't forget them. This doesn't necessarily need to be a memory technique – you could simply use a small piece of paper with your topic headings on. There is quite a difference between a small set of prompting notes, and a fully written-out speech that you deliver while staring at a stack of paper.

Assuming you do want to remember the sections, you could use one of the techniques covered previously in this book, such as an acronym of the initial letters of each area, or even an amusing poem that covers each topic in turn. What might seem like an eternity to you, as you run through it in your head to recover the next section, is unlikely to be even noticed by an audience – when talking in public we tend to hugely overestimate how much time each of our pauses lasts for. You could also use one of the advanced techniques covered in the next chapter – the memory palace technique in particular is especially appropriate for this, since you will be able to jump back into it without having to start from the beginning of the memorized list at each use of it.

LEARNING VERBATIM PASSAGES

You have your sections, and you now want to learn the contents of each in turn. Start by rehearsing the opening line for each section, and keep practicing until you can recall it as accurately as you need to. Use the repetition techniques covered earlier in the book to help reinforce what you have learned. Then once you are sure of the opening line, go on and memorize the next line or two. Once you are sure of those, go back and start from the beginning, until you can recall all of the lines together. Then keep on adding extra lines, working on just these on their own to start with, and only once you are confident of them returning to consider the whole section as a single passage.

If there are particular points in the passage where you seem to get lost each time, use one of the memory techniques from this book to help you find the connection. For example, link the final word of one sentence into the first couple of words in the next sentence in some way. Just this prompt will probably be all you need to get you going again.

VERBATIM PASSAGE MEMORIZATION

136. See how well you can memorize this extract from *Pride and Prejudice* by Jane Austen:

Chapter 1

It is a truth universally acknowledged, that a single man in possession of a good fortune, must be in want of a wife.

However little known the feelings or views of such a man may be on his first entering a neighbourhood, this truth is so well fixed in the minds of the surrounding families, that he is considered the rightful property of some one or other of their daughters.

'My dear Mr Bennet,' said his lady to him one day, 'have you heard that Netherfield Park is let at last?'

Mr Bennet replied that he had not.

'But it is,' returned she; 'for Mrs Long has just been here, and she told me all about it'.

Mr Bennet made no answer.

'Do you not want to know who has taken it?' cried his wife impatiently.

'*You* want to tell me, and I have no objection to hearing it.'

This was invitation enough.

137. The famous opening of Charles Dickens' *A Tale of Two Cities* is an interesting passage to try to memorize verbatim:

It was the best of times,
it was the worst of times,
it was the age of wisdom,
it was the age of foolishness,

it was the epoch of belief,
it was the epoch of incredulity,
it was the season of Light,
it was the season of Darkness,
it was the spring of hope,
it was the winter of despair,
we had everything before us,
we had nothing before us,
we were all going direct to Heaven,
we were all going direct the other way –
in short, the period was so far like the present period, that some of its noisiest authorities insisted on its being received, for good or for evil, in the superlative degree of comparison only.

138. You can also use verbatim memorization techniques to impress others with your knowledge. For example, you could learn Shakespeare's famous sonnet number 18, with its memorable opening line:

Shall I compare thee to a summer's day?
Thou art more lovely and more temperate:
Rough winds do shake the darling buds of May,
And summer's lease hath all too short a date:
Sometime too hot the eye of heaven shines,
And often is his gold complexion dimmed,
And every fair from fair sometime declines,
By chance, or nature's changing course untrimmed:
But thy eternal summer shall not fade,
Nor lose possession of that fair thou ow'st,
Nor shall death brag thou wand'rest in his shade,
When in eternal lines to time thou grow'st,
    So long as men can breathe or eyes can see,
    So long lives this, and this gives life to thee.

MEMORY PALACES

Have you ever gone shopping and forgotten some of the items you went out to buy, or tried to work your way through a set of tasks and then accidentally omitted to do some of them?

One particularly powerful technique for remembering lists of items is the 'memory palace' technique. This method also has the additional benefit that it can help you remember what order the items come in, although it works for unordered lists too.

Think back to a building you've visited just once or twice over the past year or so. The chances are you can remember the rough layout of that building even after just a brief visit. Can you picture the room beyond the entrance, and some of the rooms opening off it? Your memory is fantastic at this kind of recall, and perhaps annoyingly for most of us it is both effortless and not especially useful. Back in hunter-gatherer days it was a matter of life and death to be able to find your way home, or back to important places, but nowadays we have maps and satnavs, plus we tend to live sedentary lives.

Close your eyes and imagine walking around the rooms in your house. If your house is a small apartment, imagine walking around a larger property which you're familiar with. Picture the route. You come in the front door, and then where do you go? And then next? Design a route which makes sense, so it will be easy to remember it.

ENTER YOUR PALACE
Welcome to your memory palace! The rooms you are picturing, and the route you are walking, form the basis of a powerful memory technique.

Imagine that you need to remember the following shopping list:

Strawberries	Milk	Yoghurt	Cheese
Lettuce	Bread	Newspaper	Orange juice

To apply the memory technique, walk through your memory palace in your mind and deposit the objects in the rooms. The more memorably you can place each object in a room then the more memorable the item will become.

For example, you pass through your front door, noticing that the door is decorated with fresh strawberries. You enter your hall, which has milk running down all of the walls. Turning into your living room, you are surprised to see that the armchairs are made from giant yoghurt pots. You go on into the kitchen, where all of the pans are now made from hollowed-out wheels of cheese. Travelling up the stairs, you find that the steps are made from slices of bread. On the landing, the light is adorned with pieces of lettuce, and in the bedroom beyond you notice that the sheets are now made from newspaper. Moving on into the bathroom, it strikes you as unusual that orange juice is flowing from the taps!

Now, when you want to recall the list, you simply imagine walking around your house and you will find that most, if not all, of the objects come readily to mind as you imagine entering each room.

BUILD YOUR OWN PALACE

The larger your memory palace, the longer the list of items you can memorize. If the technique works for you then you can build as large a palace as you like, adding on rooms each time you work on it. You can either invent rooms, such as a swimming pool or even dog-training room, or add on parts of buildings you're already familiar with, linking them into your existing palace. It might take you time to become fully familiar with your memory palace, but you only need to build it once and then it's good for any list.

PUZZLES – MEMORY PALACE PRACTICE

139. How many of the eight items listed in the paragraph at the top of the previous page can you recall, immediately after turning to this page? Imagine walking through the memory palace as described. Make a list of what you see in each room.

140. If you didn't remember all eight objects, see if this walk through the memory palace helps: pass through the **door**, enter the **hall**, go into the **living room**, then the **kitchen**, up the **stairs**, onto the **landing** and into the **bedroom** and **bathroom**.

141. Make a note to come back and try this question in an hour or two. At that point, how many of the eight items from the trip through the memory palace at the top of page 77 can you still recall? And again tomorrow?

142. Using the same memory palace as the previous three questions, spend a minute or two memorizing the following list of items:

French loaf	Pack of mints	Apple juice
Sandwich	Magazine	Greetings card
Marmalade	Butter	

143. Try adding two rooms onto the memory palace, by adding two stages before you enter the house. Firstly, you open a gate, and then secondly you travel up a garden path, before then continuing through the door as before. Using this extended memory palace, try memorizing these ten objects. There is no need to recall them in a specific order, so you can place each object in whichever room is most memorable to you.

Pen	Dining plate	Easy chair
Kettle	Ironing board	Remote control
Flower vase	Curtain	Reading book
Painting		

144. Spend a few minutes memorizing the following twenty items using the memory palace technique, then see how many you can recall after half an hour. To remember twenty objects in ten rooms, place two objects in each room – perhaps by journeying into and then back out of the palace.

145.

146. It's trickier, but see if you can use the memory palace technique to remember the order these eight numbers are listed in:

25   84   33   98   47   52   44   36

MEMORY PEGS

A memory peg system is a method for remembering lists of information. You learn in advance a specific sequence of pegs, and then you 'hang' the information you want to remember on those pegs. By choosing appropriate pegs, and attaching the information to them in a suitable way, you give your memory a huge helping hand. You are building strong triggers to help you retrieve the information, and what's more they are in a pre-memorized order so you have no trouble recalling items in the correct order too. The pegs themselves also introduce variety, which not only connects the memories into existing concepts but also allows you to connect them in an amusing, memorable way.

Say, for example, that you want to be able to remember lists of up to ten objects. You would create a ten-peg system just the one time, and then you could use those ten pegs whenever you wanted them. The pegs are typically nouns of some type. For example you could have:

> 1: the sun
> 2: a shoe
> 3: some Brie
> 4: the floor
> 5: a bee hive
> 6: some sticks
> 7: heaven
> 8: some bait
> 9: washing line
> 10: a pen

The pegs don't have to rhyme with the numbers, but generally the more memorable the pegs themselves are the better the entire system will work.

If you now wanted to remember a shopping list of ten items, for example, we can simply connect them to the pegs. Let's say our list is:

Bread	Milk	Juice	Cereal
Rice	Apples	Butter	Salt
Coffee	Chocolate		

We can then come up with a way of hanging each one on its associated peg. For example:

1 – we could imagine some **bread** baking in the **sun**
2 – some **milk** that has been poured inside a **shoe**
3 – some orange **juice** with lumps of **Brie** floating in it. Yummy!
4 – **cereal** spilled all over the **floor**
5 – a swarm of bees collecting the **rice** and taking it back to their **bee hive**
6 – **apples** arranged in an artistic display on the end of some **sticks**
7 – an angel in **heaven** sitting down and spreading **butter** over everything
8 – going fishing with **salt** attached to the end of a line as **bait**
9 – **coffee** beans hung out to dry on a **washing line**
10 – a bar of **chocolate** signed with a **pen** to show that it's yours

The idea is that the concepts are strong enough that they become memorable. If you now read back over the pegs, since you won't have yet memorized the pegs themselves, how many of the objects above can you recall already? The pegs are:

The sun; a shoe; some Brie; the floor; a bee hive; some sticks; heaven; some bait; washing line; a pen

In this particular case the ordering isn't important, which demonstrates that we can still use the memory peg system even if we then ignore the order of the items we retrieve.

PUT UP YOUR OWN PEGS

Of course, this is just an example. You should come up with your own pegs, because only you know what is memorable and perhaps also potentially amusing to *you*. Start with just a few, and over time add more.

MEMORY PEG EXERCISES

147. How many of the ten items listed in the paragraph at the top of the previous page can you recall, immediately after turning to this page? If you have trouble remembering them, here are the pegs used in the article:

1: the sun	2: a shoe	3: some Brie
4: the floor	5: a bee hive	6: some sticks
7: heaven	8: some bait	9: washing line 10: a pen

148. If you didn't remember all ten items, turn back a page and create your own associations to attach each item to the pegs above, rather than using those given as examples, and then try again.

149. Come back and try this question in an hour or two. Can you recall all ten items? It's okay to use the list of pegs above to prompt you.

150. Using the same set of memory pegs, spend a few minutes memorizing the following list of nine yoga poses:

Cat	Eagle	Downward-facing dog
Cow face	Fish	Upward plank
Scale	Mountain	Lotus

151. Try adding two extra memory pegs. These can be whatever you like, but as suggestions you could try:

11: sticks (based on the shape)   12: shelves (based on a rhyme)

Use these extra pegs to remember the following twelve boys' names. Think of famous people, or others you know of, to put on the pegs:

Lewis	Oliver	Reuben
Oscar	Bernard	Alfie
Isaac	Zachary	Frankie
Ryan	Hugo	Teddy

152. Using your system of twelve memory pegs, see how well you can memorize these twelve pictures, and the order they are presented in:

153. Extend the memory peg system up to eighteen items. You may wish to start again, rather than using the twelve pegs so far presented – your own system is likely to be far more memorable to you.

154. Once you have prepared your eighteen-peg system, try it out with these types of food:

Pizza	Hot dog	Pretzel
Sandwich	Curry	Doughnut
Pasta	Burger	Ice cream
Noodles	Sushi	Dumplings
Kebab	Pancake	Taco
Calzone	Wrap	Chips

MEMORY PALACES WITH ADDED PEGS

The memory palace technique is a powerful memorization method, and arguably is even more useful than the peg system. After all, you can put more objects in a room than you can associate with just a single peg item.

But what if you could combine their power? If you want to remember fifty objects, you might struggle to find a good memory palace with that many rooms, so why not place some pegs in each room? In that way you potentially can combine the best features of each system.

Consider the rooms in your memory palace. Assuming they correspond to actual rooms you know of, then imagine looking around them. What do you see? Even the barest room tends to have a few items of furniture in it, so what are they? Take for example a house with a hall. In the hall you might have a door at the entrance, a doorbell ringer next to it, a key hook, maybe a radiator and perhaps a pin board, and then of course other doors or stairs and so on. It doesn't matter what the objects are, but think of five items you would see in the first room of your memory palace.

You also want to remember the order of those items, so imagine that you enter the room and slowly sweep your gaze clockwise around the room. In what order do you see those items? Now take those five items, in the order you see them, and use them as five memory pegs within that room.

Now carry on through the rest of your memory palace, putting up pegs in every room. Of course, you need only put as many pegs in as many rooms as you think you will ever need, and just as you don't need to build the entirety of your palace in a single day, so you don't need to place all your pegs immediately. But it's best to start at the entrance and work your way through the palace, rather than use a scattergun approach.

USING THE MEMORY PALACE PEGS

The first time you use your upgraded memory palace, you may find it a little tricky. But the point of this memory technique is that the palace and its pegs will then never change, or at least not very much – you may decide with practice that some pegs or rooms are less useful than others, and so to replace them with something better. But by and large you won't ever have to re-memorize the palace and the pegs, so the more you use the system the easier it will get to remember the trigger parts. Also, the more practised you get at connecting things into it, the easier and more natural it will seem.

With just a little bit of work, you can in fact build a palace that will allow you to quickly and easily remember almost any list. You can even get so fast at it that you could do it in real time, as someone reads you a list. Of course, the longer you have to place each item then the stronger the link you can build, but even just a quick thought may well be enough in many cases to allow you to later successfully recall the pegged item.

In our example of a hall, say we want to remember the following list:

Dog   Spoon   Hat   Rose   Purse

By combining both the peg and the room, we have more flexibility and hopefully more opportunities for memorable connections. So the dog could be stuck in a cat flap in the door; the spoon could be sticking out of the doorbell, vibrating each time someone pressed the buzzer; the hat could be hung on the key hook; the rose could be sitting in a pool of water that is leaking out of the radiator; and the purse could be dangling off the corner of the pin board.

The better and stronger you build your memory palace, the stronger your memorization abilities will become.

ADVANCED MEMORIZATION EXERCISE

155. See if you can remember *all* of the items on these two pages – *and* the order they are presented in. Good luck! It's all about travelling around your palace and putting everything in its correct place, neatly hung on a peg.

If you aren't yet familiar with your palace and its pegs, it's okay to make a note of them and then refer to those notes – it's the items below you're trying to remember. The palace and pegs you can learn in the future.

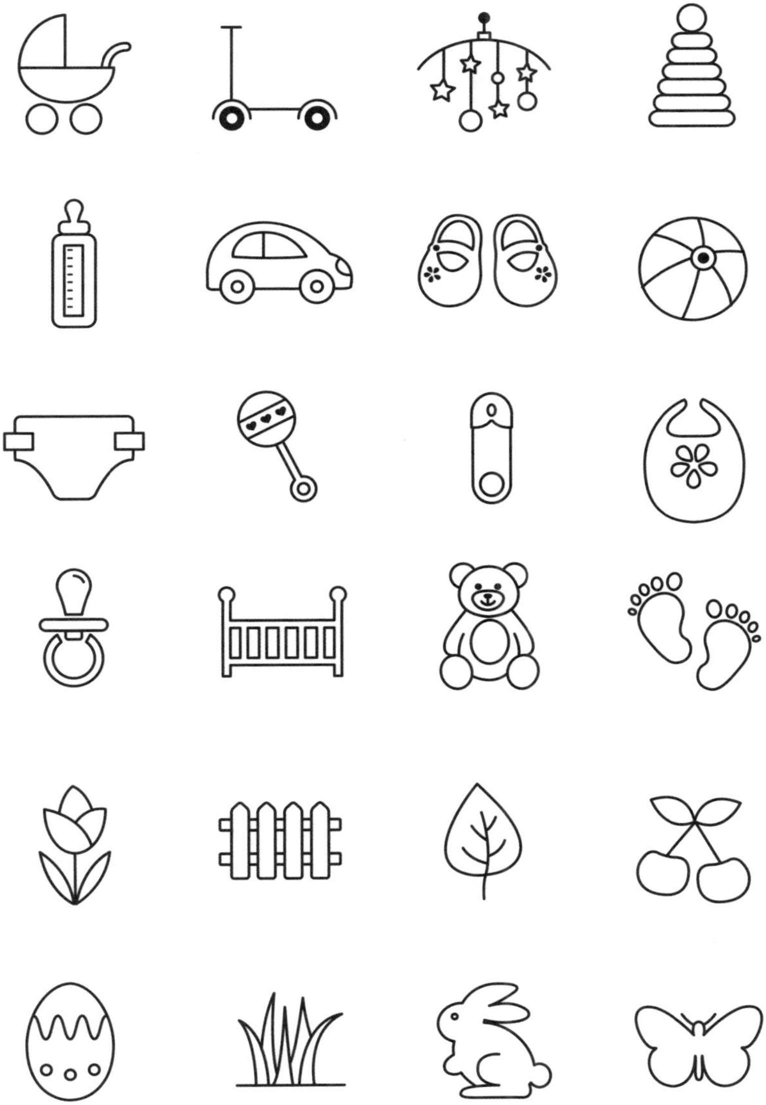

ADVANCED NUMBER MEMORIZATION

We looked previously, on pages 64–65, at specific methods for memorizing numbers. But numbers are so important in daily life that it's worth looking at some further techniques for memorizing them. The more weapons you have in your arsenal, the better disposed you will be to take on each number memorization task you encounter.

LETTERS TO NUMBERS

If you, as a one-off task, convert each letter of the alphabet into a different digit, and then learn your encoding, you can then use acronyms or acrostics to store numbers. Say for example that A=1, B=2 and so on up to I=9 and J=0, you could then also assign K=1, L=2 on to S=9, T=0, and even U=1, V=2 until you reach Z=6. You only really need to remember that A=1 and that there is a 0 to recall this sequence, since you could simply write out the alphabet to reproduce it at will.

In any case, once you have learned your system you can use the letters to remember a number. Say you have 2,859 to memorize, that would be B, L or V, followed by H or R, followed by E, O or Y, and then I or S. So if you remember 'BROS', you will be able to recall 2,859. And remembering 'BROS' is much easier than remembering the number.

With a bit of learning effort you could devise a much better letter-to-number system. In particular this one is weak for making acronyms because E, O and Y, three vowels or vowel sounds, are all used by the same number. Of course, this isn't so much of a problem for creating acrostics.

NUMBER RHYMES AND SUBSTITUTIONS

If you replace each digit with a rhyming word, you can come up with a phrase or sentence that reminds you of the number. For example, 4,378 could be 'door is free at heaven gate' – where you then ignore the words that don't rhyme with numbers. So our words rhyme with four, three, seven and eight.

Instead of rhyming words, we can also pre-learn an arbitrary number of words to associate with each digit. This can make it easier to then construct a visual memory based around a sequence of digits, by having a wider range of options to pick from. For instance we might decide in advance, when creating our system, that 'one' can be replaced by bun, jewel or dung, and 'two' by shoe, queue or peanut. We can then remember the number 1,221 by imagining a bun in a queue to obtain a shoe filled with dung.

NUMBER PEGS

The peg system covered a few pages ago is based on learning a set of items in a precise order, so those items could also be used to encode numbers in some way. For example, if your peg for 'one' is 'sun', and your peg for 'two' is 'shoe', you could remember the number 1,221 as two loaves of bread baking between two suns. If your pegs run up to 99, you can also immediately compress each pair of two digits into a single item.

NUMBERS TO SHAPES

If we want to remember not just numbers but things associated with those numbers, one method is to think of each digit as a small picture. For example, the number '1' could be a soldier standing at guard, or the number '6' could be a wheelchair. If we want to then remember that sulphur has atomic number 16, we could imagine a soldier sitting in a wheelchair with a piece of sulphuric volcanic rock. When you then want to recall this you need only remember the visual image, rather than the actual digits.

You can of course imagine each number to be many different things, so the number '6' could also be a monkey's tail or a whip, for example.

ADVANCED NUMBER MEMORIZATION

Use the methods on the previous two pages to try to memorize each of these individual numbers:

156.   957,394

157.   9,383,920

158.   45,454,938

159.   393,857,476

160.   978,465,142

161.   5,098,837,372

162.   27,648,948,395

163.   8,384,974,029,348

164.   27,945,039,985,332,482

Now try using a similar method as part of your technique for memorizing the following numbers plus their meanings:

165. Planck constant $h = 6.626070040 \times 10^{-34}$ Joule seconds

166. Gravitational constant $G = 6.67408 \times 10^{-11} \ m^3 kg^{-1} s^{-2}$

167. Elementary charge $e = 1.6021766208 \times 10^{-19}$ C

168. Electron mass $m_e = 9.10938356 \times 10^{-31}$ kg

169. Proton mass $m_p = 1.672621898 \times 10^{-27}$ kg

170. Use any number memorization techniques you like to learn this table of cubes:

2^3	=	8
3^3	=	27
4^3	=	64
5^3	=	125
6^3	=	216
7^3	=	343
8^3	=	512
9^3	=	729
10^3	=	1,000
11^3	=	1,331
12^3	=	1,728
13^3	=	2,197
14^3	=	2,744
15^3	=	3,375
16^3	=	4,096
17^3	=	4,913
18^3	=	5,832

REMEMBERING USERNAMES AND PASSWORDS

We've already covered various techniques for remembering numeric strings, such as PINs, and we also covered techniques for *creating* a memorable password back on page 45. But what if we are *presented* with essentially a nonsense string of characters that we need to remember, as does indeed happen with some online services nowadays?

The same applies to usernames, which can be randomly generated and sometimes consist of long sequences of digits. Short of writing them down, which will compromise the security these strange characters were intended to provide in the first place, what can we do?

REMEMBERING ARBITRARY CHARACTER SEQUENCES

As you might imagine, the best way to memorize an obscure sequence is to use a combination of the techniques we have already covered. So you would chunk the sequence into sections that you can make sense of, and then remember them using various memory techniques. You could then link them together with still further memory techniques.

For example, say that you have been presented with the password sequence:

M16ac95$5+

How would you go about memorizing this strange set of characters?

There are ten characters, so the first thing we would want to do is reduce the number of items there are to remember. For example, we could chunk it like this:

- M16 – similar to MI6, the spy agency James Bond belongs to, perhaps

- ac – maybe a reference to alternative current (AC) mains electricity

- 95 – Windows '95

- $5 – something that costs just $5

- + – the plus sign, which we could take to mean 'sum', 'medical help required', or countless other things

We could then link these thoughts together, so we have James Bond (at MI6, or rather M16) plugging in (via the AC mains) a Windows '95 computer and then spending $5 on a medical kit ('+') for spies. And we're almost done! We might actually now remember that obscure string of characters.

The only thing we haven't covered in our memorization list is the fact that 'ac' is in lower case, so perhaps we could remember this as **'low**-voltage' electricity. You could also use other methods to remember upper-case versus lower-case letters, so you could perhaps use names of people and places – which would be normally capitalized – to indicate capital letters, and anything non-capitalized to remember lower-case letters. It all depends on the exact sequence you are trying to remember, although if you have a lot of obscure passwords to learn it will pay to be consistent!

For symbols that aren't letters or numbers, try to connect them to their possible meanings, or what they look like. So a closing bracket could easily be a smile, as in an emoticon, or an '@' symbol could be a snail – which, incidentally, is its actual name in Italian and some other languages!

PASSWORD MEMORIZATION EXERCISES

It's good to start with easier passwords and then work towards tougher ones, so begin by finding a good way to learn each of these PINs:

171.   8474

172.   0029

173.   2847

174.   283 049

175.   938 887

176.   2849 7737

You can also try memorizing some credit card numbers – although it should be noted that these are not *actual* credit card numbers!

177.   7374 8493 3029 4945

178.   3920 3857 5729 3324 expiry 07/21 CVV code 774

Now try using the methods described on the preceding pages to memorize each of these obscure passwords:

179.   heph8974

180.   kdKjh7hh

181.   qEkdjDOdo

182.   logjsdYOW3

183.   8k8g74hs93

184.   dfhYFH!8j4

185.   sj*&orpLL

186.   plpfj8493rdjr$

187.   83ef&jd^h9+

188.   a^d@T~L#n+3*,

Next, try linking names of sites and the password for each site:

189. Clothing Master   –   hriej89klls

190. Pet Paradise   –   qriu840*^hP

191. Baby Browsing   –   Jj98&je@e~

192. Motor Mart   –   Pep8773lp#4

Finally, here are some made-up usernames for a range of sites. See if you can find a way of memorizing each of these:

193. Puzzle Mix   –   puzzmaster99@zap2mail.com

194. Brained Up   –   hdj857_cub89@fanzee44.net

195. Memory World   –   u88.mpp74@mys1t34p33p5.info

196. Bank Portal   –   ej88ejwkak998jee4

EVERYDAY MEMORY

With all of the memory techniques in this book, you should now be well prepared for the memorization requirements of day-to-day life.

Each time you are presented with something to learn, think about which of the systems you now know will be most appropriate. Even so, there may still be times when you may need other specific techniques.

KEEPING TRACK OF YOUR BELONGINGS

How many times have you failed to find your keys as you prepare to go out in something of a hurry, or have misplaced your wallet or purse and seem completely unable to find it?

Like the learned memory systems in this book, the simplest way to avoid this is to simply learn where you put things. Rather than putting them down wherever you please, use a set range of locations. And if you stop to put them down somewhere else, take a moment to focus on exactly what you are doing and make a note to your memory that is hard to forget. So link the object to the place with a humorous connection – for example, the keys are on the radiator because you have a hot date tonight and may need them then, or something similar. Whatever technique you use, the important point is to *focus* on where you put them, no matter how briefly.

REWARD YOURSELF

If you have just made good progress on a task, reward yourself. This doesn't necessarily mean eating several bars of chocolate, but it could be as simple as taking a brisk walk around the block, or stopping to check your personal email for a few minutes. Let your brain know it has done a good job, and the positive feelings will probably help reinforce the memories you just formed.

DIRECTIONS

If someone gives you spoken directions, it can be very easy to let them float in one ear and then straight out the other. The key to remembering them, of course, starts with focus and attention, and then immediate repetition after you have heard them. But more specifically, how can you go about memorizing the route given that you already know to focus and then rehearse?

If you can, ask the person giving you directions for landmarks at each step of the route. Telling you to take the second left is fine, but if they tell you to turn left at the pub that's painted bright blue, that's far more memorable and it's more likely you would remember it when you reached it, even if you forgot the actual sequence of directions itself.

If no further details are available, try translating the instructions into something more memorable. You could replace some parts, such as 'left' and 'right', with other words. So 'left' could become a reference to anything that starts with 'l', such as a llama or a lollipop, and 'r' could be a Rolls-Royce or a rat. Then if you are told to take the third left, imagine three llamas in procession crossing the road, and if it's then the first right you can picture a farmer travelling along in a Rolls-Royce behind the llamas.

Of course, doing all this fast enough while the directions are given to you may be tricky, but once you've tried it a few times you'll get much quicker as you get used to using this system. You can of course combine both methods, using a combination of real-world *and* imaginary landmarks to make the route even more memorable.

RETRACING YOUR STEPS

You might of course want to remember a route of your own devising, for example to retrace your steps to a hotel when exploring a city. In such a case very similar techniques apply, except that you probably won't need to invent details but can rather use what you actually see around you. The secret is to stop and take note of distinctive landmarks, but make sure they will also be visible when walking in the opposite direction!

EVERYDAY MEMORY EXERCISES

197. Try memorizing this 'to-do' list:

- Buy eggs
- Email sister
- Send birthday card
- Change address on bank statement
- Cancel magazine subscription
- Buy memory-training book
- Create online brain-training account
- Borrow dress from friend
- Buy tickets for concert
- Take dog for walk
- Pick up dry-cleaning
- Collect prescription from pharmacy

198. To get some practice in without any time pressure, try memorizing this list of directions:

- Go straight down the high street
- Turn left at the big supermarket
- Head on for 300 metres
- Turn right when you reach the war memorial
- When the road splits stay in the left lane
- Bear right at the traffic lights
- Keep going until you pass the duck pond
- Then it's the house with the yellow awning outside, on the left

199. Make a list of the belongings you tend to bring out with you, such as phone, camera, keys, purse, wallet, bags, car keys and so on, and then decide on a place where you will always put them when you arrive home. It could be the same place for all items if you wish.

Item   **Place**

_____

_____

_____

_____

_____

_____

_____

200. Just in case you ever need them, write down the phone numbers of some key contacts in your life – and then learn them.

Person   **Phone number**

_____

_____

_____

_____

_____

FRESH CHALLENGES

Now you've worked your way all through the book, it's time to test yourself with some additional memory challenges.

201. Can you recall the opening of *Pride and Prejudice* from puzzle 136?

202. Can you recall the opening of *A Tale of Two Cities* from puzzle 137?

203. Can you recite Shakespeare's sonnet 18, from puzzle 138?

204. Look at this arrangement of simplified faces, then cover them over and see how accurately you can redraw them in the empty circles on the following page.

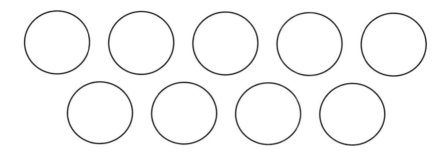

Use a memorization method to remember each of these individual numbers:

205. 958,282

206. 3,953,392

207. 33,583,392

208. 393,390,494

209. 39,955,292,503

210. 191,093,303,344

Create a simple rhyming couplet to memorize these facts:

211. Albert Einstein won the Nobel Prize for Physics in 1921

_____

212. Shimon Peres won the Nobel Peace Prize in 1994

_____

213. Use your memory skills to learn *To Autumn* by Keats:

Season of mists and mellow fruitfulness,
Close bosom-friend of the maturing sun;
Conspiring with him how to load and bless
With fruit the vines that round the thatch-eves run;
To bend with apples the moss'd cottage-trees,
And fill all fruit with ripeness to the core;
To swell the gourd, and plump the hazel shells
With a sweet kernel; to set budding more,
And still more, later flowers for the bees,
Until they think warm days will never cease,
For Summer has o'er-brimm'd their clammy cells.

Who hath not seen thee oft amid thy store?
Sometimes whoever seeks abroad may find
Thee sitting careless on a granary floor,
Thy hair soft-lifted by the winnowing wind;
Or on a half-reap'd furrow sound asleep,
Drows'd with the fume of poppies, while thy hook
Spares the next swath and all its twined flowers;
And sometimes like a gleaner thou dost keep
Steady thy laden head across a brook;
Or by a cyder-press, with patient look,
Thou watchest the last oozings hours by hours.

Where are the songs of Spring? Ay, where are they?

Think not of them, thou hast thy music too –

While barred clouds bloom the soft-dying day,

And touch the stubble-plains with rosy hue;

Then in a wailful choir the small gnats mourn

Among the river sallows, borne aloft

Or sinking as the light wind lives or dies;

And full-grown lambs loud bleat from hilly bourn;

Hedge-crickets sing; and now with treble soft

The red-breast whistles from a garden-croft;

And gathering swallows twitter in the skies.

214. See if you can memorize this sequence of Summer Olympic host countries, from 1972 through to 2016, by using a visual memory method to link the countries:

West Germany	Canada
Soviet Union	United States
South Korea	Spain
United States	Australia
Greece	China
United Kingdom	Brazil

215. The ability to visualize a memory is incredibly important to the most effective memorization strategies. So try visualizing a location you know well. Can you see it in your mind, without actually looking at it? Describe it in as much detail as you can. Then next time you visit the location, see what you think you could have added.

Initial notes

_____

_____

_____

_____

_____

_____

_____

Further observations

_____

_____

_____

_____

_____

_____

_____

_____

216. Can you still recall the capital cities of the countries from puzzles 90 to 92?

Country	Capital City
Benin	_____
Burkina Faso	_____
Cape Verde (an island)	_____
Gambia	_____
Ghana	_____
Guinea	_____
Guinea-Bissau	_____
Ivory Coast	_____
Liberia	_____
Mali	_____
Mauritania	_____
Niger	_____
Nigeria	_____
Saint Helena (an island)	_____
Senegal	_____
Sierra Leone	_____
São Tomé and Príncipe	_____
Togo	_____

217. Without referring back to puzzle 84, who were the first six Mr. Men?

218. Who were the Famous Five?

219. Who were the Secret Seven?

220. Who were the six Borrowers?

221. And again without referring back, who were the first five British Prime Ministers of the twentieth century?

222. Do you recall the host cities of the following Summer Olympics cities from puzzle 72:

1900 _____

1904 _____

1908 _____

1912 _____

1916 _____

1920 _____

1924 _____

Do you remember the passage about Lewis Carroll from puzzle 44? Try these questions:

223. How old was Lewis Carroll when he died?

224. What was the name of his guide to letter-writing?

225. Name two of his poems.

226. And name two of his books.

227. What was his real name?

228. Apart from his renown as a writer, list five other activities he was noted for.

229. Around how many letters did he write in his life?

230. What type of puzzle does the article say he popularized?

231. Where was he when he died, and what did he die of?

232. Do you recall the likelihood of a four-leafed clover from puzzle 34?

How is your memory of US Presidential history from puzzle 17?

233. Who became US President in 1881?

234. Who was the 27th US President?

235. Which two successive Presidents died on the exact same day?

236. Where was Abraham Lincoln assassinated?

237. Herbert Hoover was what number US President?

238. Who was the 20th US President?

239. What was the name of the 25th US President?

240. Who did Jefferson succeed as US President?

241. In what year did Washington become US President?

242. Who was the 16th US President?

243. Who were the first three US Presidents?

244. In what year was Abraham Lincoln assassinated?

245. In what year did William Taft become US President?

246. Who was the 31st US President?

Now retry these long-term memory exercises, from puzzles 11 to 14, with the benefit of all your later memorization experience.

247. Memorize this list of names:

David	Jennifer	Daniel
Matthew	Owen	John
Lewis	Gareth	Peter
Theo	Xavier	Sara

248. Try a similar memorization task with this list of colours:

Red	White	Mauve
Ochre	Puce	Tangerine
Blue	Scarlet	Green
Sage	Silver	Aquamarine

249. Study these pictures. How easily can you now recall them?

250. Memorize these pairs of letters:

AJ	GM	SS	XO
TX	LL	JM	BP
KL	YH	VT	ZS

251. Finally, do you recall what year Colombus 'sailed the ocean blue'? If not, take a look at page 15.

SOLUTIONS

PUZZLE 10
The letters in common are E, P, R, X, D, H and L – so there are seven letters to spot

PUZZLE 18
James Garfield

PUZZLE 19
William Taft

PUZZLE 20
John Adams and Thomas Jefferson

PUZZLE 21
Ford's Theatre

PUZZLE 22
31st

PUZZLE 23
James Garfield

PUZZLE 24
Theodore Roosevelt

PUZZLE 25
John Adams

PUZZLE 26
1789

PUZZLE 27
Abraham Lincoln

PUZZLE 28
George Washington, John Adams and Thomas Jefferson

PUZZLE 29
1865

PUZZLE 30
1913

PUZZLE 31
Herbert Hoover

PUZZLE 43
1 in 10,000

PUZZLE 47
65

PUZZLE 48
Eight or Nine Wise Words About Letter-Writing

PUZZLE 49
The Hunting of the Snark and *Jabberwocky*

PUZZLE 50
Alice's Adventures in Wonderland and *Through the Looking-Glass*

PUZZLE 51
Charles Lutwidge Dodgson

PUZZLE 52
Mathematician, logic, puzzles, deacon, photographer

PUZZLE 53
100,000

PUZZLE 54
Word ladders

PUZZLE 55
Pneumonia, in Guildford

PUZZLE 78
Days of the week

PUZZLE 79
Months

PUZZLE 80
Numbers

PUZZLE 81
Colours of the rainbow

PUZZLE 84
Mr. Tickle, Mr. Greedy, Mr. Happy, Mr. Nosey, Mr. Sneeze and Mr. Bump

PUZZLE 85
Julian, Dick, Anne, Georgina and Timmy

PUZZLE 86
Peter, Janet, Jack, Barbara, George, Pam and Colin

PUZZLE 87
Arrietty, Pod, Homily, Hendreary, Lupy and Eggletina

PUZZLE 88
Salisbury, Balfour, Campbell-Bannerman, Asquith, Lloyd George

PUZZLE 90

Benin	Porto-Novo
Burkina Faso	Ouagadougou
Cape Verde	Praia
Gambia	Banjul
Guinea	Conakry
Guinea-Bissau	Bissau
Ivory Coast	Yamoussoukro
Liberia	Monrovia
Mali	Bamako
Mauritania	Nouakchott
Niger	Niamey
Nigeria	Abuja
Saint Helena	Jamestown
Senegal	Dakar
Sierra Leone	Freetown
São Tomé...	São Tomé
Togo	Lomé

PUZZLE 98
If you rearrange the spaces, the sequence 1989 1990 1991 is revealed

PUZZLE 133
Chloe, Samuel and Jemima

PUZZLE 134
Samuel, Kimmy and Victor

PUZZLE 216
See solution to puzzle 90

PUZZLE 217–221
See solutions to puzzles 84–88

PUZZLE 222
See puzzle 72

PUZZLE 223–231
See solutions to puzzles 47–55

PUZZLE 232
1 in 10,000

PUZZLE 233–246
See solutions to puzzles 18–31

PUZZLE 251
1492